BEING INTIMATE
A GUIDE TO SUCCESSFUL
RELATIONSHIPS

John Amodeo, Ph.D. practices psychotherapy and couples counseling in the San Francisco Bay Area. He is an adjunct professor at Sonoma State University and is licensed as a Marriage, Family, and Child Counselor.

Kris Amodeo, M.A. is a registered Marriage, Family, and Child Counseling Intern, practicing in the Bay Area. They both specialize in work with individuals and couples regarding intimacy issues. Together they lead workshops and groups designed to facilitate personal growth and interpersonal contact.

JOHN AND KRIS AMODEO

BEING INTIMATE

A GUIDE TO SUCCESSFUL
RELATIONSHIPS

ARKANA
LONDON AND NEW YORK

First published in 1986 by Arkana Paperbacks
Arkana Paperbacks is an imprint of
Routledge & Kegan Paul Inc.
in association with Methuen Inc.
29 West 35th Street, New York, NY 10001

Published in Great Britain by
Routledge & Kegan Paul plc
11 New Fetter Lane, London EC4P 4EE

Set in 10 on 11 Sabon
by Input Typesetting Ltd, London
and printed in Great Britain
by Cox & Wyman Ltd
Reading, Berks

Library of Congress Cataloging in Publication Data

Amodeo, John, 1949–

Being intimate.
Bibliography: p.
Includes index.
1. Intimacy (Psychology)   2. Interpersonal relations.
3. Insight in psychotherapy.   I. Amodeo, Kris.   II. Title.
BF575.I5A46   1986   158'.2   86–3608

British Library CIP Data also available

ISBN 1–85063–037–2

Dedicated with gratitude to our primary teachers, without whose wise guidance and encouragement over the years, this book would not have been possible: William Andrew, Karen Bohan, Rose Breda, Edward Chalfant, Peter Campbell, Ken Cohen, Ignacio Gotz, Bob Kantor, Frank Lambasa, Ed McMahon, Sylvia Randall, Neil Selden, Roger Walsh, and Bernard Weitzman.

Contents

Acknowledgments ix
Introduction 1

PART I: THE DILEMMA
1 Who's living your life? 7
2 The romantic myths we live by 14

PART II: THE WAY OUT
3 Opening to felt experience 27
4 The willingness to be vulnerable 36
5 Focusing: a process of being with our felt experience 43
6 The Focusing steps 52
7 Replacing the inner critic with an inner caretaker 66

PART III:
TOWARD THE EXPERIENCE OF LOVE AND INTIMACY
8 Trust: a foundation for intimacy 83
9 Self-revealing communication: a vital bridge between
  two worlds 109
10 A guide to effective communication 121
11 Working with anger 136
12 Toward a new perspective on commitment and
  marriage 144
13 Betrayal and beyond 158
14 Conclusion: implications for a world at peace 162

APPENDIXES
A The Focusing steps 167
B Troubleshooting reference guide 170
C Tips for the Focusing guide 176
D A guide to initiating relationships 183

E A guide to improving relationships   186
F Additional suggestions for couples or friends who
   want to Focus together   189
G A guide to separating   193
H Some words that convey feelings   196
I A guide to resources   199

Notes   203

Bibliography   206

Index   209

Acknowledgments

We would like to give special thanks to the following people for their generous support and assistance with the manuscript: Bess Amodeo, Susan Amodeo, Hill Eshbach, Joan Kloehn, Steven Ruddell, Mary Tedesco, and Bob Zelman.

We also want to express our appreciation to the following individuals for their unique contributions:
Americ Azevedo, Peter Campbell, Anna Climenhaga, Dick Dina, Neil Dinkin, Barbara Easterlin, Eugene Gendlin, Meryll Gobler, Joseph Goldstein, Roy Harris, Elliott Isenberg, Tom Heller, Jack Kornfield, Dick Martin, Michael Mayer, Bob Mendelsohn, Brad Parks, Kent Poey, Ernie Shermán, Tom Schlesinger, Ann Weiser, John Welwood, and John White.

Introduction

Our counseling experience with individuals and couples provides us with a privileged view into an ordinarily hidden dimension of people's lives. Those courageous ones who are willing to see things as they are and acknowledge the dissatisfaction and unhappiness in their lives offer precious glimpses into the more hidden fears, hopes, and concerns faced by all of us to one degree or another. Those utilizing counseling and psychotherapy services are often the braver ones among us. Far from being weak or somehow 'sick' (stigmas that are rapidly changing as our society matures), they possess the strength to ask for assistance with difficult problems that interfere with being happy and developing satisfying sources of love and intimacy.

In the following pages, we will discuss what it takes to grow as a human being. We define personal growth as a lifelong process of ever more fully coming to know ourselves and others. Such growth involves developing a more intimate connection with ourselves and with those around us. As we grow more in touch with the depths of ourselves, we develop greater confidence in our power to risk giving and receiving love. In addition, as we learn to accept ourselves and recognize personal needs that must be fulfilled in order to feel more whole, we grow toward the realization of our human potential for peace of mind, greater aliveness, and deeper wisdom regarding the meaning and direction of our lives.

We grow through facing and skillfully dealing with conflicts and difficulties that arise in relation to living our lives and, particularly, in regard to creating and sustaining intimate relationships. Throughout this book, we will offer insight and direction relevant to initiating and developing intimate relationships and meaningful friendships. Our comments will be based on personal experience and upon observations culled from thousands of hours spent with individuals and couples exploring obstacles to the creation of successful relationships. In their struggles to make the internal and external changes necessary to discover genuine love and intimacy, their rich experience offers hope and inspiration for us all.

The book includes segments of therapy sessions that illustrate key points. For the sake of clarity, we may, at times, condense several sessions' worth of work, or share vignettes from different sessions (in all cases, people's names have been changed).

The experiential tool that forms the foundation of this book and our private counseling work, groups, and intimacy workshops is called 'Focusing.' This approach to personal growth is based upon extensive research conducted by Eugene Gendlin at the University of Chicago into the key elements that make psychotherapy effective. As a result of his achievements in this area, Dr Gendlin received the Distinguished Psychologist of the Year Award bestowed by the Clinical Division of the American Psychological Association.

Based upon his research, Gendlin distilled several key steps that can be taught to those seeking positive changes. He has written a helpful book called *Focusing* (1981), describing this approach. Later, we will explain Focusing in our own way, and describe the experiential steps as we teach them so that you will have them available if you want to learn Focusing. In addition, we will show how the Focusing process can provide a crucial foundation for the development of lasting intimate relationships. By offering a helpful structure through which to contact our real feelings, Focusing can gently take us to a place inside ourselves where we are simultaneously in touch with the depths of our own being and the depths of another person.

Although we will do our best to explain how to Focus, it would be unrealistic to expect to learn it fully through the written word alone. We present it here to convey the direction in which you will need to grow (or continue to grow) in order to experience the greater love and intimacy you want. After completing the text, you may wish to consult the Guide to Resources in the back of the book. This offers opportunities for further guidance and experiential training that complements what is offered in this book.

Part I begins by exploring the dilemma that most of us find ourselves in as a result of having been influenced by a society that has encouraged us to avoid and deny our real feelings. Part II offers a way out of this predicament through describing the process of Focusing and re-connecting with the depths of our actual felt experience. Part III discusses essential factors that form the foundation for developing successful, intimate relationships. These include how to develop trust, ways to communicate more effectively, and learning how to be kindly disposed toward our feelings. In this section, we also offer reflections on commitment and marriage – topics that generate many questions, concerns, and hopes.

The appendices consist of additional guidelines for using the Focusing process with yourself or another person. Additional guides are also provided that may be used for assistance in initiating a relationship, improving an existing one, or separating from one. These appendices have been included as a reference guide to encourage you to explore your own personal concerns and conflicts as they arise. Growth and change are hardly possible through a mere intellectual understanding. Effectively exploring how you feel about your life and relationships leads to the growth of an inner awareness – a bodily felt insight – that is vitally necessary for experiencing greater love and intimacy. Whether you want to initiate an intimate relationship, enjoy richer contact with a present partner or friend, or separate with maximum learning and minimum pain, it is our hope that the following pages will contribute to your capacity to develop and maintain deeply satisfying relationships.

PART I

The dilemma

CHAPTER 1
Who's living your life?

Recognizing that all is not well – that our lives are not as fulfilling and meaningful as they could be – is the beginning of wisdom for many people. This recognition is often a difficult one, especially if those around us are silently conspiring to insist that 'everything is just great.' However, this basic acknowledgment can become a vital doorway to an astonishingly rich dimension of meaning, vitality, and happiness. The simple perception that we are, at least to some degree, dissatisfied, or that we could be happier in our lives and relationships, can become a pathway toward the fulfillment and peace of mind that is our birthright.

Our high-pressured, depersonalized society provides very little support for us to take the time necessary to understand ourselves to the degree that is essential for living a genuinely happy life. Our formal education neglects the task of teaching us the skills required to develop enduring love and intimacy. Additionally, very few of us grow up in a home environment that fosters a capacity to know our own feelings, communicate them effectively, and listen deeply to another's experience.

Sadly lacking in the wisdom and skills necessary to initiate and sustain meaningful relationships, individuals grow up without these abilities. Regrettably, they then become the insufficiently educated parents, teachers, and leaders for the next generation. And so the cycle continues.

As you will see, a major key to establishing meaningful relationships is to become aware of what you want, and recognize certain changes that need to happen inside yourself in order to actualize these wants and preferences. Accomplishing this requires an ability to affirm yourself by honoring the precious feelings and needs that lie at the very depths of who you are as a human being. Learning to contact and respect these genuine feelings, without capitulating to punishing self-criticisms and self-invalidations, you can begin naturally to move toward ever-richer dimensions of love and intimacy. Before doing so, however, it may be helpful to recognize the extent to which you may have lost contact with yourself and with your genuine feelings and needs.

THE PROCESS OF LOSING TOUCH WITH OURSELVES

From our very birth, we are extremely dependent upon others. The human infant depends upon the parents for survival for a longer period than any other species. It has also become increasingly clear that infants and children are highly dependent upon their parents for emotional development. Being deprived of positive emotional contact leads to frustration, anxiety, and withdrawal, as well as greater difficulty for the infant to progress smoothly to its next stages of development.

Since the infant is unable to communicate its numerous physical and emotional needs, many of them go unmet. All parents have felt the frustration of not knowing what their screaming baby wants. In addition, parents, however saintly they may be, cannot possibly fulfill all of the plentiful demands placed upon them. As a result, the infant experiences the periodic terror of being totally alone, isolated, and vulnerable, and periodic rage toward the world for not satisfying all of its needs.

As the infant becomes a child, the need for love and belonging continues to be primary. Since the child is wholly dependent upon the parents to meet these needs, their wishes and opinions become all important. This fundamental reliance upon the good graces of cooperating adults reflects the extraordinary extent to which parents and other significant figures hold power over children. Facing the possibility of being disliked or unloved is a frightening prospect for a defenseless child. Disapproval is felt as a painful rejection. Continual rejection may be experienced as a cruel denial of one's basic right to exist, unless one 'shapes up' or 'behaves oneself.'

Being incapable of standing alone as a separate individual,

the youngster's sense of well-being depends upon validation and support from others. Lack of approval or damaging punishment can deal a terrible blow to his or her self-esteem and developmental progress. Withheld affection can arouse extreme anxiety as the young individual desperately struggles to gain a sense of love and approval. Chronic disapproval can lead to severe depression as the child gives up hope. These cycles of anxiety and despair can form the basis for a frustrating pattern that, if unresolved, can persist throughout adulthood.

A child's attitudes, feelings, and actions are largely shaped by the wishes and demands of significant adults, particularly the parents. Since a child does not possess the capacity to tolerate sustained disapproval, he or she must learn to adopt attitudes and behaviors that are sanctioned – and to eliminate those that face the threat of condemnation. For example, many individuals in our society, especially women, learned that anger is not permitted – expressing it led to punishment or isolation. Similarly, many men were taught that feeling sad or hurt demonstrates weakness and is therefore bad. Repeated messages of this sort induce the vulnerable child to find ways of avoiding unacceptable feelings; they learn to 'toughen up' in a world defined by adults. Before long, through a remarkable ability to adapt to the hostile demands of the environment, the young person successfully learns not even to feel, let alone express, emotions and impulses that are displeasing to significant others.

In order to further insure that this adaptive structure survives, we adopt a set of ideas that reinforce and offer justification for the repression of our feelings. For example, if we have been persistently told 'only babies cry,' or that only bad children get angry, then whenever we begin to experience such feelings we hold them down through the newly found power of self-critical thoughts and beliefs. These cognitions may produce an inner voice that tells us how to behave and when to 'control ourselves.' The development of this controlling 'internal dialogue,' or 'inner critic,' coupled with a muscular armoring or contraction within the very tissues of our bodies, is the price we pay to satisfy our overriding need for acceptance and approval. If we have been taught to deny anger, for instance, then in situations where anger would tend to be the natural human response (such as when we feel abused, oppressed, or unseen by others), we may sink into an introverted sadness or depression. When young, this may be accompanied by thoughts such as 'I'm a bad boy if I get angry,' or 'if they find out I'll be spanked.' As adults, these thoughts may become more sophisticated and complex. For example, we may say to ourselves, 'I'm being overly sensitive, I shouldn't react so strongly' or 'this isn't worth getting upset about,' or 'these people are just impossible to deal with – they'll never understand me.' As a result of these rationalizations, our natural bodily impulse to express the anger is held back – stifling vitality, producing guilt, and reinforcing the self-image that there must be something wrong with us. Over time, this can lead to chronic depression, where our feelings are literally 'pressed in,' and we are left feeling hopeless, numb, lethargic, or unsure of ourselves.

Another typical pattern that develops as a result of denying our real feelings is to mask an underlying fear or sadness with anger or stoic emotional control. 'Real' men, for instance, get angry but, like John Wayne or Clint Eastwood, they know no fear, even while bullets are whizzing past their ears. When circumstances arise that would normally elicit fear or hurt, there may be an instantaneous rage reaction that stirs up a smoke screen to protect us from more threatening emotions. For example, instead of acknowledging anxiety, regret, or dissatisfaction regarding our lives, we may resent our spouse for not satisfying our every need, as if that were his or her responsibility. Or we may insulate ourselves from others by assuming an excessive degree of responsibility for our well-being.

This type of person learns to avoid softer feelings through becoming a 'rugged individual,' or what we teasingly refer to as a 'responsibility athlete.' They are exemplified by the upwardly mobile corporate executives who believe that life is a solitary struggle for survival. Asking for help is viewed as a weakness; needing support is embarrassing and threatening. An example of a more subtle embodiment of this desire to control feelings are the animated graduates of weekend seminars who believe that they completely create their own reality through the power of their single-minded intention.

Fearing dependency, these individuals maintain separateness through a stance that psychologists refer to as 'counterdependence.' In other words, there is so much fear of needing someone or becoming dependent that the individual reacts by developing beliefs and behaviors that insure a 'safe' distance from others.

Although the need for acceptance and support as children may be readily admitted, we may hesitate to recognize that our emotional vulnerabilities do not end with the arrival of adulthood. We still want to be liked. We are still very concerned with people's opinions of us. We still want to be loved, accepted, and part of the team.

The advertising industry is well aware of our adult vulnerabilities. Profiting by exploiting our frustrated desire for love and approval, corporations skillfully design ads and persuasive television campaigns that prey upon our fears and dissatisfactions. Assisted by industrial psychologists, corporations fill the media with messages that tell us what we need in order to be accepted, well-liked, or successful: if only we would purchase the latest brand of toothpaste, cigarettes, slacks, or automobile, we would finally attract the love, approval, or sexual fulfillment that we have always wanted. We may like to think that we are beyond such attempts to be manipulated by the advertising media; however, if that were true, corporations would not spend billions of dollars each year persuading us to buy their merchandise. There is a product designed to assuage any conceivable dissatisfaction. And if we get a headache trying to decide which one to buy, there is a product to meet that need too.

As we grow up, a certain kind of inner intelligence guides us toward survival and away from threat. Our character gradually stabilizes in a way that enables us to bypass emotions and avoid experiences that might meet with disapproval. We learn attitudes and behaviors that increase the likelihood of being liked and respected by others. Personality patterns become firmly established at an early age and then we conveniently forget the whole process that brought us to this sad point of insulation from our real feelings and needs. 'That's just the way I am,' we often say. Actually, that is how we have become due to compelling environmental forces largely outside our control. Succumbing to these, we are no longer living our own lives. We have lost touch with the depths of our real feelings and lost contact with those things in life that are truly important to us. No wonder we are confused and frustrated – unsure of what we really want and bewildered about how to find the peace of mind we desire.

Our emotional vulnerabilities and, perhaps, physical survival have caused us to abandon ourselves.

Positive change begins with the sobering awareness that instead of fully living our lives, we are often conducting the kind of lives that others have urged us to live. We can re-connect with a dormant source of meaning and joy as we realize that we have slowly and unknowingly entered into a secret agreement with society at large. Becoming aware of how we have silently conspired together to remain within a domain of rigid rules, constricting social roles, and approved ways of feeling and behaving, we can begin to find a way out of the confines of this sad predicament. Then, rather than continuing to perpetuate a lifestyle that disallows contact with our actual feelings, wants, and interests, we can begin to feel freer and more alive through taking the first step of sensing and honoring how we really feel inside.

Many individuals finally become willing to face the fact that they are out of touch with themselves after having failed to cope with a traumatic event or an insistent series of disappointments. A stressful career change, sudden illness, loss of a loved one, separation, or threat of divorce can reveal the poverty of our once-reliable defenses. Dashed hopes, repeated frustrations, or compelling fears can instigate a crumbling of the old assumptions upon which our stable perception of reality has been based. As a result, we enter a period of being 'in between' world views – we have temporarily lost our ground. Our old self-image and sense of reality is reluctantly seen as inadequate to deal with the crisis at hand.

This painful period can be a very creative one if we allow our once-necessary defenses to remain suspended and courageously face our current situation. Then, instead of avoiding the crisis or struggling to control things through our will power, we can use this period to explore personal feelings and meanings that may have been too frightening to face directly, but that are now necessary to explore in order to grow.

The arrival of a difficult crisis is not the only impetus toward a process of personal growth. We may choose to take charge of our lives before minor discontents snowball into an emergency situation. In either case, positive directions can unfold as we learn to 'go with' our fluid inner process. Opening ourselves to what is real in our lives, we become more comfortable being ourselves.

Each juncture along the path of self-discovery can be felt as a step toward less inner tension, reduced interpersonal conflict, and a greater sense of freedom and happiness. As we come to allow feelings that arise within us to be heard, understood, and expressed, we develop a relationship of acceptance toward all that we really are. We find that feelings that were once scary or threatening contain an integrity and wisdom that can lead us in positive directions. As a result, we begin to feel increasingly alive and real. As we become more and more released from our historical conditioning, we begin to live our own lives and find relationships with those who are growing similarly. The possibilities for alive, spontaneous intimacy then open in a deeper way than we might ever have imagined.

CHAPTER 2
The romantic myths we live by

One of the most unfortunate ways in which we have lost contact with our real feelings and needs results from the effects of internalizing cultural myths and images regarding romantic love. Romantic images portrayed in popular fairy tales, songs, stories, plays, movies, and advertisements, fill our minds and hearts with compelling ideas and unreal expectations regarding love.

Beginning with our impressionable pre-school years, we are exposed to a series of enchanting fairy tales about wondrous characters such as Cinderella and Prince Charming. Then, as we become adolescents thirsting for knowledge and understanding, the media exposes us to additional romantic scenarios that provide unrealistic models for what to expect and how to develop an intimate relationship. This input leaves us with strong psychological imprints regarding future possibilities that we then desire and search for. Imprinted with a fixed set of anticipations regarding the kind of magical person who we expect will bring us abundant love and unending happiness, we learn to compare each man or woman we meet with an idealized image of the kind of mate we want – someone who will passionately sweep us off our feet and with whom we will live happily ever after.

Observed signs that match our conditioned images include physical features such as height, physique, hair style, manner of dress, social status, and capacity to care for us financially. We may also be attracted to those who treat us in the polite, courteous manner afforded a prince or princess despite how they may really feel toward us.

Upon meeting one who resembles these deeply internalized images of a hoped-for mate, we may experience a sense of 'falling in love.' This occurs, in part, as a result of the close interplay between powerful emotional and physiological energies and our culturally worshipped images and beliefs. An exciting rush of passions may then suddenly pour forth in relation to one who fits our desired image.

Falsely believing that the path to love and fulfillment lies in the actualization of our romantic quest, we look for one who corresponds to our images of love, beauty, strength, or whatever attributes awaken our deeper longings. In reality, when we finally discover such a fascinating person, he or she may be elusive and hard to contact. On the surface we may be allured or captivated, but, since on a deeper level we do not really know the person, we can project all kinds of noble virtues that the individual does not really possess. We unwittingly attribute these deeper qualities to the other person when he or she fits the pictures that we falsely assume are associated with these desirable traits.

'Falling in love' with such a person, we are often intoxicated with our own romantic hopes about living happily ever after now that we have finally found someone who resembles our images. Our feelings of 'being in love' are manufactured ones insofar as they stem from our treasured images. Genuine intimacy, on the other hand, derives from authentic contact with another human being who possesses both strengths and limitations.

A woman, for example, may be looking for the charming, handsome prince whose image has been firmly ingrained in her mind. She may believe that finding this special person will guarantee her a permanent supply of love. This sought-after individual may also need to embody comforting qualities reminiscent of her 'good' father, or he may have to possess characteristics she always wanted in a father, but never had (such as a capacity to protect her). Unfortunately, such expectations (whether conscious or not) involve a surrender of her personal power and autonomy. Depending upon a man for her well-being, she may then experience little self-worth or life meaning apart from the relationship.

Men, on the other hand, may be on the lookout for their beautiful princess – a fair and tender maiden who they can protect and be loved by. This myth reflects the image of the

Prince Charming type – the 'good boy' or the strong macho man looking for a gentle woman who will shower him with unending love, recognition, and nurturance. Unfortunately, such a man is mostly in love with his images of love. His unwillingness to accept the woman as an autonomous and equal individual or disclose his own feelings and weaknesses reveals a fundamental lack of awareness of what it takes to develop an enduring sense of intimacy.

Soon after 'falling in love' in these ways, there follows an inevitable crash well known to those of us who have abruptly fallen out of love. We take a hard fall as our romantic hopes and expectations are dashed upon the rocky shores of reality. For example, a woman who is driven by the search for an idealized man may feel disappointed to observe unanticipated 'weaknesses' in him, such as feelings of fear or sadness. Confused or threatened by this discovery, she may reject him as insufficiently 'strong' to meet her needs. In a more updated idealization, a woman may want a man who is able to vulnerably share his feelings. While this is a step forward, there may still be difficulty when the man actually displays the vulnerability that she supposedly wants. For instance, if he is awkward or faltering in his self-expression, he may be rejected.

Conversely, a man may be disappointed to discover that his once-adored female companion occasionally gets angry or disagrees with him. In short, he becomes disturbed or outraged because she has a mind of her own, and a set of feelings that are different from his and, therefore, threatening to his desire to meet his needs by controlling her. A more contemporary man may view himself as being beyond such narrow idealizations; he may think he wants an independent woman. In reality, however, his conditioned sense of masculinity may continue to be threatened by a woman who actually *is* powerful and outspoken.

Becoming involved with enticing people who evoke feelings of elation or excitement rarely bears fruit when based upon romantic images that lack real grounding or substance. Intimate contact requires us to be in touch with our real feelings – those that exist prior to (or beneath) these socially conditioned myths and images. Genuine love and intimacy are often difficult to attain, in fact, because we are frequently unable to distinguish our actual experience from secondary experience that arises out of these culturally generated imprints. Massive confusion and dissatisfaction result from this incapacity to differentiate our original feelings and needs from those learned as we were growing up.

Before we can overcome the alienating effects of these socially conditioned romantic myths that have become an integral part of our operating philosophy of life, we must first identify the nature of these myths, and notice how they have subtly influenced our way of relating to a prospective mate or present partner. By re-evaluating these romantic beliefs, we may begin to replace them with more realistic understandings that are more likely to lead to the successful relationships we want.

ONCE IN LOVE, ALWAYS IN LOVE

One popular element of romantic myths is that once we 'fall' in love with a person, we will be forever in love with that person. In addition, if we truly love someone, we will do anything it takes to keep the relationship intact, however abused, mistreated, or ignored we may be. 'True love,' in this view, amounts to symbiotically clinging to a person. Even if he or she left us long ago, we will forever await his or her return.

This unrealistic belief accounts for much of the torment experienced in relationships in which love is unreciprocated. Becoming desperately attached to a solitary source of love, we set ourselves up for considerable pain and disappointment if the other person is not inclined to respond favorably.

An unreciprocated involvement often looks ridiculous to those who can clearly see the futility of our predicament. 'Being in love,' however (or believing we are in love), we remain preoccupied with thoughts, feelings, and images of the other person. Such an attachment can persist even though we receive clear verbal statements, or obvious nonverbal messages (expressed through their actions) that they are unwilling or emotionally unable to be with us. Stubbornly refusing to accept the reality of another's disinterest or lack of desire to work things through, we may continue to profess our love. We may also deceive ourselves with the hope that some magical change may bring them back into our arms. Clinging to these thin strands of hope, we compromise our integrity and postpone living our lives.

Unable to sway another person, we may feel ashamed, or berate ourselves for failing. Condemning ourselves for not getting what we want, we may fall prey to a self-esteem tailspin that can negatively impact all aspects of our lives as we retreat from a world increasingly seen as hostile or dangerous.

By clinging to an unattainable person, we become an emotional captive, painfully attached to the experience of desire or longing, which we misidentify as love. We may derive gratification for maintaining this identification by perceiving ourselves as the determined heroes who will not easily give up the noble quest to remain true to the one we love; such tales of unrequited love are glamorized in literature and contemporary movies.

Exclusively depending upon one other individual for our sense of self-esteem and personhood, we become an emotional hostage to that person. Having unwisely opted to surrender to this individual before a realistic sense of trust has had time gradually to develop in the natural give and take of relating to one another, we suddenly find ourselves at the mercy of his or her whims and preferences. Our position is one of helplessness resulting from the powerful effects of unrealistic romantic myths coupled with the poverty of inner resources to effectively care for ourselves.

Letting go of our romantic attachments is often difficult because such images are infused with powerful emotional energies and propensities for loving that we innately possess. These tendencies of our organism, however, exist prior to our learned myths and images. As we discern and become familiar with our innate capacities, we can begin to create genuinely loving and intimate relationships based upon a more fundamental dimension of our humanness. First, however, we must be willing to bravely face reality and grieve the loss of someone we cannot have, as well as relinquish our innocent romantic notions.

THERE IS ONLY ONE PERSON I CAN DEEPLY LOVE IN MY LIFETIME

Closely associated with the notion 'once in love, always in love,' is the idea that there is but one other person to love in our lives; and, once we find such a person, all our needs will be met. This magical notion manifests as the romantic search for the ideal mate – the one who will somehow relieve our sorrow, allay our loneliness, and provide ongoing nuturing and love; such an idealized person is sometimes called our 'soul mate.'

Looking for a person who matches these romantic fantasies can lead to a very long wait. Blinded by our search and expectations, we can easily overlook those who may be quite capable of giving at least some degree of love and support. Withdrawing from those around us or new people we meet because they do not correspond to our mental pictures, we might miss the very opportunity that could lead to the deeper levels of love and contact we want. As a result, we remain isolated because we fail to accept a flawed prince or princess, that is, a human being. Actually, we overlook the fact that all people, including ourselves, possess human weaknesses and limitations, and that by accepting a person inclusive of these limitations, he or she may gradually blossom into the loving, caring person we might like to be with. The 'right chemistry' between ourselves and another person may then arise in a more gradual manner as we become better acquainted with his or her depths and more deeply in touch with ourselves.

The unrealistic notion that there is only one person for us in this lifetime may return to haunt us once we think we have located such an individual. We then expect to be totally happy for the rest of our lives because we have now found the man or woman of our dreams. When this scenario does not materialize, we may become upset with our spouse for somehow causing the problem or blame ourselves for the unhappy outcome.

Exploring the cause of a faltering or failed relationship, we may be hard pressed to understand what went wrong. Unfortunately, many of us never learned the simple fact that finding a mate does not ensure happiness. A successful relationship requires considerable work, primarily regarding our own personal growth. The romantic myths we grew up with ignored the fact that we first need to grow as autonomous individuals (at least to some reasonable degree), before we can sustain a meaningful primary commitment with another. Also, unless we become well-acquainted with ourselves – knowing our feelings and affirming our needs, and learning to communicate these in responsible ways, we will form the unwise habit of depending upon another to furnish us with well-being. Looking toward another to make us feel content or whole, we fail to be realistically responsible for our lives. Placing this heavy burden on another can eventually smother the life of a relationship or lead us to be disgusted with ourselves for relying too heavily upon another.

Believing that there is only one possible partner or source of love in our lives leaves us isolated and deprives us of the contact that is available through other friendships. In addition, if the relationship or marriage breaks up due to unresolved differences or the death of our partner, we may feel condemned to a lonely existence for our remaining years. The underlying romantic belief that may hook us here is, 'If I really loved him or her, I could never give myself to another person.' For example, in *The Thornbirds*, a popular book and television mini-series, the main character, Maggie, spent most of her life longing for a priest who was emotionally and physically unavailable to her. While his attraction to her and professed love added fuel to her own passions, he was not willing to offer the unreserved, committed kind of love that she wanted. Re-stimulated by his periodic visits, she developed an intense attachment that she was unable or unwilling to disengage from. This painful addiction led to much sorrow and isolation, embellished by the romantic notion that she loved only him and, therefore, could never consider surrendering to another man.

Caught by the power of such a compelling myth, we may irrationally imagine that we are betraying a person by loving someone else, even though the desired partner may be dead or otherwise unavailable. Actually, we would only be betraying the saccharine romantic myth that is ruthlessly controlling our lives. Until we re-evaluate the insidious myths we live by and replace them with more suitable ways of thinking and living, we will continue to be manipulated by them and thus guarantee a life of needless frustration, isolation, and heartbreak.

EXPERIENCING NEGATIVE FEELINGS MEANS I AM NO LONGER IN LOVE

One of the most destructive romantic myths is that if we truly love someone, we should never experience 'negative' feelings in relation to that person. 'Negative' feelings, that is, ones that most of us have been taught to avoid, such as anger, hurt, or fear, are viewed as bad or threatening. Experiencing or expressing such feelings is seen as indicating that something is terribly wrong with the relationship, or that our love is no longer true. The one toward whom we have such feelings may also interpret our displayed emotions as a sign that we never really loved him or her. After all, according to this belief, how can we feel angry or sad if we are 'really' in love?

This narrow-minded 'black and white' thinking imposes a heavy burden on us. Pushing aside unwanted feelings in order to salvage what we believe to be true love – that is, a love unblemished by 'lowly' emotions – is a sadly futile and counter-productive task. As unpleasant emotions arise (as they inevitably do) we may conclude that this person is not 'right' for us. Or, as a result of years of repressing unwanted emotions, the interpersonal contact may become so devoid of real feeling that divorce may seem to be the only viable option.

Being naive about the workings of human emotions and what they really mean, we may recognize no alternative other than to avoid these feelings. This can lead to unfortunate consequences in terms of our personal growth, the nurturing potential of the relationship, and even our own physical health. One woman, for instance, who complained of getting headaches and being chronically tired, stated in the course of therapy, 'I'm tired of being criticized by my husband.' Never standing up for herself, she gradually realized that her physical symptoms were related to taking in his criticism and then carrying it around inside herself with no effective outlet for her pent-up frustrations. Exploring the matter further, she realized that she was actually very angry about his criticisms and lack of support. Soon after contacting her anger, however, this emotion quickly disappeared. When asked what was happening inside, she said, 'If I let myself be angry, I feel that I'd be betraying my husband.' Since anger, for this woman, meant a lack of faithfulness, she quickly bypassed her anger whenever she would begin to feel it. Thinking in categories of 'right or wrong,' and 'good or bad,' she had difficulty holding the perspective that she could be angry and still love her husband. Observing her unconsciously operating beliefs about anger and love, she realized how unrealistic it was to assume that feeling angry meant that she did not love her husband. Glimpsing the ill effects of this belief for the first time, she could begin to explore the possibility of honoring her legitimate feelings of anger without the accompanying self-condemnation.

Equating negative feelings with an absence of love, we spend considerable energy protecting one another from facing potentially threatening feelings. We may withhold the truth, change the topic of conversation, or even lie in order to do what we consider to be a favor to the other person – namely, to shield him or her from those feelings that he or she was also trained to avoid. For example, we may feel angry or hurt because our sexual needs are not being met by our partner. Instead of discussing the matter, we may just grin and bear it. However, the long-term consequence of withholding our discontents is to stifle the natural flow of feelings that keep a relationship thriving. No matter how hard we may try to cover up our true emotions, they eventually leak out or burst open. We may, for instance, express our anger in passive ways, such as by being late or buying things with our shared money. Or we may seek out an affair in order to meet an essential need that is not being satisfied at home.

The romantic myths that lead us to protect others from our unpleasant feelings can never lead to the happiness we want. Feelings have a life of their own whether we like it or not. They will simply find substitute outlets – ones that can do more harm because we are often unaware of them. In addition, the practical effect of protecting others from 'negative' feelings is to insulate them from feelings themselves. The inability or unwillingness to open to painful feelings has the inevitable effect of diminishing our positive feelings as well. In other words, our ability to access feelings in general becomes blocked. Therefore, protecting others from the natural doses of hurt or pain that accompany our lives is to deprive them of enjoying the pleasure and happiness that could come if we chose to honor and deal with all of our feelings.

In reality, love is not some sterile, remote phenomenon existing separately from our everyday lives and emotions. Instead, it is to be found in the midst of our daily lives. As we will see later, emotions such as sorrow, hurt, anger, and remorse can become a vital pathway toward a more deeply and genuinely felt love and intimacy.

Recognizing the noxious effects of alluring and seemingly innocent romantic myths can provide a sobering antidote that can begin to free us to face reality more directly and courageously. Although we may fear that this will bring a life devoid of romance, the good news is that the transition to a reality-based approach to relationships provides a needed foundation for the growth of an inspiring dimension of love and intimacy. Qualities we consider romantic – such as love, caring, excitement, joy, and wonder – can take on fresh dimensions of meaning and be cherished in a new way as we replace romantic myths with a more workable perspective that embraces our human limitations.

PART II

The way out

CHAPTER 3
Opening to felt experience

The solution to many of our discontents lies in the direction of re-discovering our actual experience. The phrase we will use to describe this core dimension of being is 'felt experience.' We also refer to it as 'organismic experience' because it is an ongoing process of our very organism. This process underlies our very existence in the world. It is always accessible to us, whether or not we are conscious of it in any given moment.

Felt experience refers to an awareness of that which is directly experienced inside us without the mediating influence of thoughts, beliefs, judgments, or intellectual analysis. It includes feelings, emotions, and sensations that arise from within us. They may be distinguished by the fact that our bodies register these inner events. Although we are often unaware of the ongoing flow of these experiences, they can be felt within ourselves in a very concrete, immediate way. For instance, we may feel in our bodies a tightness or fluttering that characterizes fear, a heaviness or pressure that reflects sadness, or a tingling or energetic sensation that expresses a feeling of excitement. In short, our very organism is continually in the process of experiencing; we can allow ourselves to feel this in a very simple, direct way.

Pleasant or uplifting events can be more readily enjoyed as we contact this fundamental dimension of organismic experience, apart from the interfering tendencies of our active minds. An example of being in touch with ourselves in this way is when we are totally engrossed in the experience of a beautiful sunset. A striking sunset seizes our attention immediately. We do not need to think about it or analyze why we are struck with such beauty or inspiration – we simply are.

Being fully open and present to the sunset, apart from our mental associations to it, we might notice a bodily felt component to our experience, such as a quickening heartbeat, a deep sigh, or a feeling of lightness that reflects a sense of serenity. Such a rich experience may be difficult, if not impossible, to express in words; we might use terms such as 'beauty' or 'fullness' or 'awe' to express how we feel inside. Words can never fully convey our subtly felt experiences; as such, communicating our experience to another person is always fraught with difficulty.

There is a very thin line between being present to our felt experience of the moment and reverting to our familiar mode of rational analysis or verbal descriptions that are disconnected from our immediate feelings. For example, instead of simply being with the awesome experience of the sunset, we might compare it to other sunsets or become preoccupied with thoughts such as, 'This is a pretty sunset,' or 'I wish there were fewer clouds in the sky.' As such thoughts enter, we partially lose our rich experience of the moment. It becomes obscured as we succumb to our usual mental functioning, subject to its tendency to compare, evaluate, or analyze. These faculties of mind certainly have their place; they help us survive in the world. But by overly identifying with them we become somewhat removed from our organism's immediate registering of essential experience.

Felt experience thus arises in relation to the immediacy of everyday life events. Work situations, relationships, or health concerns may give rise to a surge of sharp, urgent impulses that we refer to as feelings or emotions. These may arise in a variety of felt tones, and be expressed by words such as excitement, terror, despair, enthusiasm, rage, humiliation, or isolation. Or, we may notice quieter feelings mildly flowing through us that may be symbolized by words that reflect less intense feeling tones, such as regret, annoyance, discomfort, uneasiness, embarrassment, shyness, or satisfaction. Sensing a full range of fundamental emotions and feelings connects us with a rich dimension of felt experience.

Organismic experience may also include a dimension that may be referred to as 'meaning.' Our deeper feelings often contain an important message or a certain kind of wisdom. When tapped, this wisdom holds the promise of a more fulfilling life. Such meaning or wisdom exists within the context of current feelings and life situations. At first, we are usually uncertain regarding the messages these feelings and circumstances hold for us. As we learn to open to felt experience in a welcoming way, it can begin to speak to us more clearly.

For example, if you feel a vague queasiness in your stomach and allow yourself to quietly experience that apart from your usual thoughts about it, the unique meaning contained in this feeling may begin to slowly emerge. The meaning could be anything, since it arises from the extraordinary complexity that characterizes your life. For example, you may notice that this queasiness has to do with an uncertainty about whether your interest in getting to know a well-liked person is reciprocal. This may remind you of a need for loving contact and a fear of being alone. Or, perhaps this queasiness reflects a fear that if you express a discontent to a friend, you may be rejected. You may then realize that you fear rejection because you take it to mean that you are an undesirable person or that you are a failure. Exploring further, it may suddenly dawn on you that you are a worthwhile person even if this particular individual fails to appreciate you fully. Or, you may realize that you need to be willing to be alone, rather than stifle your real feelings and betray your integrity for the sake of maintaining someone's approval.

Becoming aware of previously neglected felt experience and noticing related meanings tends to move us in the direction of feeling better. We feel relieved because we are now beginning to hear the messages that our bodies, in their own way (in the best way they know how), are trying to convey. Sensing these meanings, we feel more deeply connected with ourselves and with the positive direction of our lives.

EXPERIENCING OUR NEEDS

Sustaining direct contact with felt experience, we tend to notice a certain band of that experience that may be termed 'needs,' or, more precisely, felt needs, since this refers to a felt dimension of experience. Felt needs can sometimes be distinguished by a certain urgency behind them. Hunger, for example, is a clearcut experience that is universally understood. We may also notice more subtle bodily felt experiences, such as a dull ache in the pit of our stomach, or a heavy feeling throughout our body. If we pay attention to such feelings, instead of distracting ourselves from them, a word such as 'loneliness' may best express how we feel. Remaining aware of this feeling, we may notice a corresponding need to make meaningful contact with another human being – that is, to experience a sense of acceptance and intimacy. Honoring the various needs that arise out of our felt experience, and learning how to best fulfill the full spectrum of our human needs, is a crucial part of the art of living.

Felt needs contain a kind of intelligence, which, when accurately understood and acted upon, can move us in a direction that feels 'right,' 'meaningful,' or 'natural' – that is, toward the realization of our greater human potential. Learning to understand the language through which our needs make themselves known is a crucial preliminary step toward their satisfaction, and, hence, toward the possibility of furthering our growth as human beings.

Sigmund Freud and his followers were among the first to recognize that our basic needs and impulses were different from, and often in conflict with, our more accustomed thoughts and systems of beliefs. Abraham Maslow, a pioneer of Humanistic and, later, Transpersonal Psychology, elaborated this rudimentary insight by identifying a hierarchy of basic human needs that he discovered during the course of twenty years of personality study.

The most basic needs, as described by Maslow (1968), are physiological ones. These include the need for food, water, and sleep. The next level of needs are safety needs, as for example, the need for shelter and an environment free of physical threat. The third category of needs are referred to as 'belongingness' needs. These involve the desire to feel accepted – secure in the knowledge that we have a safe place in the world. Following this, we tend to want human affection and close loving relationships. The next category discovered by Maslow consists of esteem needs – the sense of being respected by others and having positive regard for oneself.

The failure to experience the fulfillment of these fundamental needs can account for ongoing dis-ease and conflict. Those who learn to meet their needs successfully become happy, healthy people. Those who are unable to do so tend to be dominated by insecurity, confusion, anxiety, depression, or isolation. They remain part of the mass of people who, in the words of Henry David Thoreau, lead lives of 'quiet desperation.'

Feeling gratified in our basic needs frees us to pursue further aspirations. The human spirit consistently strives to reach beyond its present limitations in order to fulfill what Maslow calls 'growth needs' or 'self-actualization needs.' These deeper longings involve a calling to fulfill our full human potential – the more sublime aspects of our being. These include the development of creative talents, meaningful vocations, and, perhaps, most importantly, a progressively deeper realization of our human capacity for joy, well-being, and interpersonal fulfillment.

As we move toward the relative satisfaction of our basic needs, and as we approach the 'farther reaches of human nature,' as Maslow (1971) entitled his final book, the quality of our lives and relationships transforms in positive ways. As we grow toward maintaining consistent contact with felt experience, and meeting needs that arise out of it, we enter a richer dimension of intimate contact with ourselves, other people, and life itself.

The intention of this book is to provide guidance and support so that individuals may learn to enter the stream of their own personal experience in order to move toward meeting basic needs for love and self-esteem, and beyond that, toward meeting growth needs that lead to even greater self-actualization and fulfillment in our relationships. Our hope is that by describing some of the scenery observed by others along the way, familiar landmarks may be recognized that will provide guidance and encouragement to our readers.

The foundation for such a journey takes shape as we begin to uncover our readily available, though frequently obscured, felt experience. Only then can we contact our real needs and discover, in our own way, how best to fulfill the calling these felt needs represent. As we do so, a pathway toward the actualization of our deepest human and spiritual aspirations naturally unfolds.

Being out of touch with our needs, we often seek substitutes that only partially satisfy our deeper yearnings. For instance, many people join social groups or religious organizations in order to meet the need to belong. However, underlying longings for a more personalized affection and intimacy may then go unnoticed and remain unnourished. Or, we may be told that our longings merely reflect some selfish desire that must be suppressed or transcended. Of course, trying to deny our felt desires only creates the additional desire to get rid of them. This confounds our unhappiness through bypassing the wise messages reflected in our deeper longings. If we can courageously honor our innermost experience, even though our peer groups or those in authority do not appreciate this deeper soul-searching, then a doorway may open to a rich dimension of our inner world.

The rewards we may achieve through pursuing career achievements, accumulating wealth, or being entertaining and humorous may provide a faint glimmer of the fulfillment that is possible if we could confront the full force of our actual needs and remove obstacles to satisfying them in a more straightforward way. It is often a startling discovery to realize that love and closeness are not dependent upon our worldly achievements or social popularity. The ability to be our real selves with just one other person can lead to a depth of contact that is far more rewarding than being widely venerated by large audiences who do not really know us. The compulsive search for fame or power is an empty substitute for the simple need for intimacy and love.

Acknowledging the lack of love and intimate contact with others may be so threatening to face that we may take comfort in mind-dulling habits and addictions that include alcohol, overeating, overworking, or watching television. The operating principle becomes: if I am unable or unwilling to satisfy my needs, then I must find a quick way to obliterate the experience of these painfully unsatisfied longings. Recognizing the self-defeating quality of our indirect efforts to gain approval, love, and contact can empower us to discover how to fulfill these needs more directly. And realizing that emotionally dulling addictions are separating us from realizing our deeper needs may motivate us to give them up. As we begin to trust ourselves to enter the stream of our organismic experience, we may find the guidance we need to relinquish what is not working for us and move toward actualizing our greater potential. Before doing so, however, the initial step in this growth process is to affirm the basic right to *have* these needs in the first place, as well as the right and the responsibility to learn how to fulfill them. The famous statement of Rabbi Hillel says it well: 'If I am not for myself, who will be for me? If I am only for myself, *what* am I?' Although we may quickly distract ourselves from feelings that may threaten us, our organism, in its never-ending struggle to grow according to nature's blueprint, persistently tries to reveal its true growth needs. If we are equally persistent in turning a deaf ear to these organismic needs and feelings, our bodies may eventually revolt in the ways they are programmed to rebel – through anxiety, stress, mild physical symptoms or even debilitating illnesses. It is as if our bodies were saying, 'If you don't take care of me, I can't take care of you.'

A typical way in which this denial of the right to our needs manifests is in terms of feeling unworthy of love. This disempowering feeling often has roots deeply buried in the past. Exposed to disappointments, abuse, or criticism for not meeting parental or societal expectations, we may begin to believe that there is something terribly (though indefinably) wrong with us. Internalizing hurtful judgments from others, or believing, as children, that we were the cause of our parents' upsets or divorce, we may have unfairly concluded that we are somehow unlovable. We may also have received the unspoken message that we must work hard to earn love by conforming to others' expectations. Thinking that we are unacceptable, we may have concluded that we had better hide our needs or eliminate them entirely. In fact, our survival as children may have been aided by this self-protective stance.

In addition to feeling undeserving of love, we may also stifle ourselves through the unfortunate belief that wanting love is a sign of selfishness, and must therefore be shunned in favor of the more noble virtue of offering love to others. This austere belief, when carried to its logical conclusion, leads to a society in which everyone is busy trying to give love, but nobody is available to receive it. The value of being loving is rather meaningless if others do not have the capacity to deeply receive and feel the love that is freely given.

Cultural and religious beliefs often encourage us to deny our basic needs, or, to say this in another way, to deny the wholeness of our being. As a result of this self-denial, we may become 'need numb' as we lose touch with our needs entirely and thereby lose our emotional grounding in the world. Of course our needs still do exist, which accounts for why those who deny them continue to be plagued by vague discontents, habitual self-criticisms, ill-defined worries, or unsettling dreams. Reaffirming the basic right to our needs and learning how to meet them skillfully without becoming emotionally enslaved to any particular individual is a vitally empowering step towards finding ourselves, feeling more alive, and growing as a person. A case in point may illustrate this.

Robert came to therapy complaining about a lack of meaning in his job and life. After a few sessions he revealed that he had no in-depth relationship, but that he liked it that way because he resented being dependent. Exploring further, he acknowledged that past relationships had ended in disappointment, with one woman criticizing him for being too insensitive and another one dissatisfied because he was too needy and 'wimpy.' Feeling bewildered and hurt by these conflicting messages, he chose not to get too close to anyone and, instead, to take care of himself. However, his vague discontent betrayed the fact that he was not taking care of his real need for love and caring contact.

As he began to experience his real needs during the course of therapy, he could no longer deny that he wanted deeper intimacy in his life. However, reaching out to another person involved a willingness to let go of control and to accept the risk that he might get hurt if he began to live more in his felt experience. The central issue of his therapy then revolved around learning how to be more at ease with this ever-present possibility of being hurt (instead of rigidly bracing himself against it). He also experienced relief to recognize that others' reactions to him were simply *their* reactions, which he had absolutely no control over and which did not necessarily mean there was something terribly wrong with him.

Basic needs are ever-insistent. If they are invalidated or unmet, we are left with continuing discomfort and unfulfillment, or a vague, uneasy background feeling that reflects the fact that something is sadly amiss in our lives. Through listening to the wisdom contained in these feelings, we may learn directly to acknowledge our real needs despite whatever inconvenience, discomfort, or pain this may first bring about.

By honoring our organismic experience as an ongoing process that can become a friend, we may learn to translate its many messages (in the form of feelings, emotions, and vaguely felt intuitions) in order to better meet our real needs. Befriending our experience in this manner can be facilitated by a courageous willingness to be vulnerably present to unfamiliar feelings and unpredictable situations.

CHAPTER 4
The willingness to be vulnerable

Recognizing that the need for love and caring contact is a universal one, we may be bewildered to observe ourselves or others keeping it a closely guarded secret. But the sad fact remains that most people tend to feel ashamed or embarrassed to directly acknowledge their needs for love and intimacy. This is largely because society teaches us that having such needs is a sign of 'weakness.' Acknowledging these needs to ourselves or communicating them to others can be terrifying because it places us in the precarious position of being susceptible to rejection or humiliation. This outcome is an ever-present possibility, particularly because exposing our needs may intimidate those who are struggling to ignore their own felt needs.

Validating our growth needs and affirming our prerogative to fulfill them requires a willingness to live with an essential quality of vulnerability and uncertainty. The necessity to be vulnerable in order to grow is often difficult to recognize; in fact, at first, it may appear to be in direct conflict with our need to protect ourselves from physical vulnerabilities that threaten our survival. Ensuring physical well-being often requires that we be in control to one degree or another in order to function in the world. However, if we similarly try to be in control in relation to meeting our needs for love and closeness, we will quickly stifle the autonomy of others, and thus smother intimacy.

In my (John) capacity as a consultant doing psychotherapy with police officers, I frequently observe difficulties with issues regarding intimate relationships. I am frequently asked the question, 'If I learn to let go of control, how will I be able to function on my job?' The solution lies in realizing that it is not all or nothing – absolute control or no control – which means learning to live with a certain quality of flexibility.

Such jobs as repairing machinery, keeping records, performing surgery, or programming computers require an ability to execute tasks in a precise fashion. On the other hand, the path of building trust and enjoying the experience of love and intimacy is facilitated by an ability to relinquish our usual efforts to control things. This requires that we allow ourselves to be humanly vulnerable rather than pretend to know all the answers or try to control the behavior of those with whom we want to feel close. The decision to risk relinquishing control opens us to potentially scary consequences because we are called upon to learn a function that appears to be in direct conflict with traits that seem necessary to survive and operate effectively in the world.

Growing up in our culture, most of us have learned to be in control not only for the sake of physical survival, but for emotional survival as well. Unfortunately, this habit of control then dominates our lives outside of the office – extending into our intimate relationships and friendships. We then need to explore why we feel so unsafe with another human being who longs for the same tender contact and love that we so much want.

As we practice contacting and expressing our real feelings and needs where it is safest – with a spouse, friend, or therapist – we can grow in ways that then enable us to be more relaxed and open in our daily lives. As we progress in this direction, we may even find that our jobs can be accomplished just as effectively, if not more so, by adopting a more relaxed attitude. We may also feel freer to express our viewpoints regarding how the workplace can become a more satisfying environment. A growing trend, in fact, is for corporations to consider employees' input so that they may feel a greater sense of enrichment and meaning in relation to their work.[1] As more individuals begin to feel at home in their vulnerability, they will work toward creating environments that foster personal growth and a cohesive sense of community. As values such as honest communication, mutual respect, and shared decision-making become more appreciated, we will slowly evolve toward a society where our personal lives can be more harmonious with our work lives.

Until society values the creation of environments that make it safer for us to be vulnerable in the world, our task is to become more open where we feel reasonably secure, and then grow from there, reaching out to test the waters beyond our safe circle. This growth process, however, must begin with a recognition of our basic vulnerability. Avoiding this by closing off our felt experience, we bypass the doorway that could lead to the fulfillment we desire.

As we open to felt experience, we soon discover that our human existence is a vulnerable one in that we are closely interconnected with others. The fact that we need love and closeness, however, does not guarantee that we will receive it from a specific individual. Since everyone possesses free choice, each person has the capacity to withhold or withdraw love. Each has the power to act in ways that may lead to our being hurt (whether intentionally or inadvertently). As such, being vulnerable is basic to the human condition, however firmly we may resist or struggle to maintain control over our lives and emotions.

Expressing this dilemma in another way, it is apparent that we all want to feel cherished for who we are, without having to resort to pretensions or manipulations. However, the bind we are in is that we can also be rejected for who we are. Being ourselves and boldly stepping out into the world means letting go of control over how others may feel about us. Of course, in reality, we have absolutely no control over other people's reactions to our unguarded inner selves, or whether they will give us the acceptance, respect, and love we want.

Although we may put on a happy face or cover up what we imagine to be faults, many people have an uncanny ability to perceive the substance beneath the style. Some individuals who are scared of their own felt experience may prefer us to be cautious, indirect, or restrained. Frightened by our honesty and directness, they may reject us. Others, however, who are closer to self-actualization (and, as such, have a greater capacity to really love us), may resent or mistrust our propensity to hide feelings, withhold the truth, or manipulate in order to gain approval. In such instances, we may be rejected not because people dislike who we are, but because we are not allowing ourselves to fully be who we really are. Sorting out the varying reasons for these two types of rejection may teach us the importance of developing a clearer sense of to whom we can reveal our most tender feelings.

Rather than deciding to shield our vulnerability from everyone, and thus close off any possibility of creating a genuinely intimate relationship, we may choose to understand the conditions under which we feel safe to begin trusting another person. Then, even though we remain vulnerable to being wounded, we can minimize this possibility by making wise choices regarding the people with whom we associate. Intimacy may then gradually grow as we monitor the degree to which we feel safe revealing our real selves to another individual.

REINTEGRATING THE INNER CHILD

Once we begin to recognize and remove layers of conditioned thoughts, cultural beliefs, and romantic images that have obscured our felt experience, we discover more and more of our fundamental openness in relation to other people and the world. An apt metaphor to describe this openness of being is that of the innocent child. Such a child is one who is alive and playfully present in the world without recourse to pretensions or manipulations. The child lives in the here and now and is in touch with a spontaneous pleasure in relation to unfolding life events; he or she predominantly lives in the organismic realm of feeling, sensing, and being. In contrast, the typical adult is non-vulnerable, cautious, deliberate, and serious, and tends to spend more time living in the mental realm of thinking, strategizing, defending, and evaluating.

Children are also less self-conscious, which can be observed through their direct and uninhibited eye contact. In addition, there is often a disarming tenderness and sensitivity in relation to others. Unlike the majority of adults, the child is also wonder-filled, and in close touch with some essential quality of being or life essence. This is aptly reflected in the Biblical verse inviting us to become like little children in order to enter the Kingdom of Heaven.

We do not wish to romanticize children as psychologically superior to adults. For instance, in the early stages of growth, they tend to be more intent on satisfying their own needs rather than being sensitive to the concerns of others. However, the healthy child is not apologetic or defensive about his or her needs and feelings, and it could be argued that with skillful parenting, plentiful love, and non-judgmental communication (balanced with appropriate expressions of parental feelings and needs), the child would naturally grow toward a mature recognition of the needs of others. In fact, attempting to force children to become unselfish before they naturally become so results in the creation of a personality compulsively trying to meet needs that have never been adequately met (psychologists refer to such a character structure as a 'narcissistic personality'). In any case, we use the word 'child' or 'inner child' merely as a metaphor to describe the vulnerable, open, soft part of ourselves.

One of the more noteworthy aspects of children (before the ill effects of social conditioning set in) is their innate ability to receive love. They delight in absorbing genuine expressions of affection without feeling guilt, reluctance, or unworthiness. This innocent, natural facility to receive nurturing can transform, in adulthood, into a blossoming of a wise vulnerability that can receive (as well as give) in an increasingly conscious, direct, and intimate way.

Honestly facing the fact that we are not receiving the depth of love and contact we need is quite painful and often terrifying. The challenge of adulthood is, in part, to become comfortable with once again being vulnerable enough to honor a full range of needs and discover how to fulfill them in ways that lead to growth.

Opening to our basic vulnerability, and the accompanying feelings that inevitably follow, we are brought face-to-face with our desire for love and intimacy. Being conscious of these needs, rather than dismissing them as a bother or inconvenience, we can then live our lives with an eye toward having them satisfied when appropriate circumstances arise. In short, we can learn to receive contact and love through being present to meeting our needs and opening to those who we sense may be able to satisfy them.

It is a sorrowful human tragedy, whether due to lack of

education, a failure of courage, or an unfamiliarity with available assistance, to realize that so many people have spent so much time isolated, anxious, or depressed – alienated from real needs, hopes, and aspirations. No matter what stage of life we happen to find ourselves in, however, we can begin to regain contact with our lost vulnerability. Having compassion for ourselves, we may recapture that spontaneous delight in being alive – a feeling that can continue to grow and expand as we overcome obstacles to more directly receiving nurturance and love.

As we become more comfortable in our wise, childlike vulnerability, our perception of the world begins to alter and sharpen. Being in closer contact with ourselves, we tend to perceive others more freshly and clearly. We can more easily discern those who are narrowly identified with limiting belief systems and those who have abandoned their autonomy for the security of identifying with some group. We can then more clearly notice those who are living closer to their vulnerable core of felt experience – self-directed individuals living their own lives. As we learn, through experience, to make wiser discriminations, our choices regarding who we spend time with can become more selective and better attuned to our felt needs. As a result, we will choose to be with those who we feel nurtured by, rather than those with whom we feel abused, unappreciated, or unloved.

Allowing our vulnerable inner child to emerge awakens a dormant joy and aliveness. But, along with an increased sensitivity to life, we face a greater possibility of being wounded if our childlike openness is met with judgments, rejections, or personal attacks. It is the very effort to avoid such painful feelings that prompts us to evade our needs, betray our experience, and create a lifestyle to protect us from the dreaded experience of hurt.

The simple act of allowing ourselves to become as vulnerable as we actually are opens a door to receiving love and being intimate. However, there are obvious risks involved. We may then be confronted with the unfamiliar realm of our yet untapped inner world, including turbulent emotions, unexplored terrors, accumulated hurts, unclear meanings, and other vaguely felt impulses and feelings. What is commonly termed 'personal growth' is largely a matter of becoming better acquainted with this world and increasingly friendly toward it. We will then become less frightened by it, and gradually learn to draw strength and sustenance from the resources that lie dormant within us. As we are then faced with threatening life situations, we will become increasingly confident that we can experience and deal with whatever arises within us as a result of being vulnerably present in these situations. As we come to friendlier terms with the 'shadow' side of our being, we may come to discover a precious dimension of peace, wisdom, and joyful aliveness awaiting us within the deeper realms of our inner world.

The Focusing process provides a helpful structure through which to open to our presently felt experience and understand whatever gems of meaning may be lying dormant within that experience. Through encouraging an attitude of acceptance and gentleness toward all aspects of ourselves, we can touch our experience in a new way and proceed to understand the wisdom contained within it. As we come to know and appreciate ourselves with increasing clarity and compassion, we can realize ever-greater fulfillment and meaning in our significant relationships. As we learn to become more intimately acquainted with ourselves – more vulnerably present to our actual felt experience – we actualize our potential to create lasting intimacy with others.

CHAPTER 5

Focusing: a process of being with our felt experience

The Focusing process was developed in the mid–1960s by Eugene Gendlin and other psychological researchers at the University of Chicago. They asked a simple question: 'Does psychotherapy really help people, and, if so, what is happening inside those who are progressing?' Through analyzing thousands of therapist-client sessions recorded on tape, they discovered that individuals achieved positive results to the degree that they were able to be in direct contact with their felt experience. The researchers found that after just one or two sessions, they could accurately predict whether therapy would succeed or fail. Despite whatever technique of therapy was used, positive changes occurred through the client's capacity to be present to his or her experience. Individuals who did not have this ability to sense themselves inwardly would not reap therapeutic gains, even after years of therapy.

Gendlin spent years ascertaining the central steps that enabled these gifted individuals to contact their felt experience in a way that led to growth. He then began teaching these steps to others, and, through receiving feedback, he continued to refine them in order to maximize their simplicity and effectiveness. Further research confirmed the possibility of effectively teaching these skills to those who ordinarily would make little or no therapeutic progress.

The essence of the Focusing process is to sense from the inside our actual experience as it is occurring in the present moment. More specifically, Focusing involves attending to our felt experience of a particular problem or meaningful life issue. At first, our experiential sense of a personal concern or life situation will be vague or 'fuzzy.' As we stay 'Focused' on this unclear sense, we can become progressively clearer about what we are feeling. And as we do, whatever meanings these feelings may have – whatever messages they may hold for us – have an opportunity to be heard.

Gendlin referred to this unclear experiential sense of personal concerns as a 'bodily felt sense,' or simply, 'felt sense.' The word 'bodily' refers to the fact that our experience is physically felt. Whether we are aware of it or not, our personal concerns, life events, and interpersonal encounters are registered in a bodily way. Taking time to Focus on the bodily felt component of unresolved matters is a primary means of becoming more attuned to our experience. Doing so often leads to a resolution of difficulties and a release of accumulated physically held tension. Focusing can bring out what is most real and most precious about us by inviting us to be in touch with the depths of ourselves in a caring, friendly way. Through its gentle, non-pressuring approach, the Focusing process helps us be present to a full spectrum of feelings in a way that does not overwhelm or debilitate us. As we feel safe to open to our felt experience as it currently exists, ever-deeper aspects of that experience – subtle felt senses – have an opportunity to emerge.

Our felt sense of an issue goes deeper than our more readily accessible feelings. For instance, as we begin to become aware of our felt experience of a particular concern or situation, we may first notice familiar feelings such as anger or frustration. However, our felt sense is more subtle than the emotions we may be accustomed to; it resides quietly beneath these surface level feelings – awaiting our patient, sustained attention before becoming clearer to us. For example, some people find it easy to feel sadness, while others are comfortable expressing anger without guilt or hesitation. Allowing ourselves to be aware of such emotions is often a crucial first step toward a resolution; however, we are likely to remain stuck in the same repetitive, unproductive cycles until we are willing to risk looking further. For instance, we may freely express anger, but never really grow because we get repeatedly caught up in the same recurring pattern of emotional build-up and release. We may temporarily feel better as a result of the emotional discharge, yet never discover deeper feelings or elusive meanings that keep perpetuating the cycle. The steps of Focusing can help us become clearer and more resolved by bringing us in closer touch with an underlying dimension of felt experience – our bodily felt sense. A case in point may further illustrate this.

Bill would feel instantly angry whenever Julie mentioned that her sexual needs were not being met. He *knew* he was angry, but that was as far as it went. When he finally Focused on his feelings regarding her dissatisfaction, something new emerged. At first, the familiar anger was there. Staying with how the anger felt inside his body, he experienced it as a heaviness in his chest, which then shifted into a tightness in his neck. Experiencing the tightness in relation to his situation, the word 'frustrated' arose to express his present feeling. It then occurred to him that he truly wanted to please her, but just did not know how to do so. Discovering that he was more frustrated than angry, he began to feel some inner release. And beginning to realize what this frustration was really about (that he did not know how to satisfy her), was a 'felt meaning' that produced a further relaxation in regard to this difficult issue. However, still feeling tense inside, he continued to Focus. He could sense that something more wanted to be experienced or understood. After a few minutes of being with his bodily felt sense of frustration, he noticed a queasy feeling in his stomach. Focusing on the felt sense of 'queasiness,' it then occurred to him that he felt an aversion to acknowledging her dissatisfaction because he interpreted it as meaning that he was a failure. Focusing on the felt sense of being a failure then produced a deeper release as he realized that he did not need to be so harsh on himself by judging his self-worth according to her experience of his sexual performance. As a result, he felt more of a willingness to listen to Julie, as well as share his own feelings.

As this example illustrates, our felt sense includes subtle feelings and bodily sensations that often go unnoticed. Our immediate feelings and emotions exist in a wider context; they have to do with this or that concern that is vitally meaningful to us – such as the need to affirm our self-worth in the above example. As such, our initial feelings provide a doorway into an ever richer dimension of our lives. As Bill continued Focusing in subsequent sessions, other issues emerged, such as his difficulty discussing concerns that might bring up painful feelings for himself or Julie. As he now began to face issues that he had previously avoided, he began to grow in new ways because he could *feel* the new realizations that were coming to him – they were not just intriguing ideas. He could sense the quiet excitement and bodily release that resulted from being with his experience and sensing its meaning from the inside.

The bodily felt release that may ensue from Focusing is termed a 'felt shift.' This involves a noticeable change in how we are experiencing a life issue; it is a physiological release that can be felt. We may, for instance, feel lighter or freer. Or we may sigh and take a deep breath as some inner pressure diminishes. This inwardly felt shift that results from effective Focusing has been scientifically measured in biofeedback studies as a distinct change in brain wave patterns, signifying a more relaxed state of being.[1]

We may experience a shift even though the concrete circumstances of a particular situation remain the same. Whether these circumstances change or not, we can feel better. It is usually our *relationship* to a life situation or concern that keeps us stuck, not the circumstances themselves. Our situation may, and often does, change as our manner of carrying it inside us begins to shift. But the external change springs from an inner shift of attitude or perspective, rather than from the effort to control circumstances or manipulate people.

We will now present an additional example to try to convey more of a 'feel' for how the Focusing process works. As I (John) am Focusing, I feel some discontent regarding a relationship. As I begin to explore it, I experience a heavy feeling in my chest. I then notice a sense of feeling hurt. It is not just an isolated, disconnected hurt – it has to do with this immediate relationship. I know that there is something about this relationship that leaves me with this heavy feeling, but I have no idea yet what it is. My felt sense is vague, blurry, fuzzy. This is the nature of the felt sense. I know I'm on track. I know that if I am patient enough and allow myself to openly experience this general, all-encompassing feeling of heaviness, it will begin to tell me something of itself. The intelligence it contains will disclose itself.

I now allow my attention to remain inside my body as I experience this sense of heaviness. Being gently aware of what I am experiencing can give rise to new perspectives, unexpected feelings, and fresh meanings. I wait. I know that the first things that come are often self-comforting ideas or mental judgments such as, 'she's very self-centered,' or, 'if only she would change.' I recognize these as criticisms that never help the situation. Even if I am right, they do absolutely nothing to help me feel better. Resolution will come only as I allow my inner experience of felt sensing to unfold and express itself – not through trying to 'straighten her out' or change her in some way.

As I let go of these outer directed thoughts and criticisms, I return my attention to the bodily felt sense of heaviness, noticing if something more wants to come. I wait. A minute or so passes.

Focusing is, in a sense, a meditative process. It involves an active willingness to listen. It is based on the trust that we have an inner sense of knowing, which, as we learn to tap it, can guide our lives toward greater joy, freedom, peace of mind, and loving contact. The doorway toward embodying these qualities lies in our capacity to touch and welcome our felt experience.

As I continue to wait and remain with a felt sense of heaviness regarding the relationship, something finally comes: I don't feel appreciated. Yes, that expresses it well. I notice the beginning of a 'felt shift' – a changed sense of how I am carrying this issue. My chest begins to feel lighter.

This tension-relieving felt shift begins to happen as I remain friendly toward my inner feelings and allow 'felt meanings' to emerge. Having practiced Focusing, I know that a shift comes in its own time; it is beyond my usual efforts to control reality. But I can prepare the ground so that I enter an inner environment where a felt shift is more likely to occur. By Focusing properly, the ground is being prepared.

Expectations regarding a desired outcome often get in the way of Focusing. However, if we anticipate remaining stuck, without any hope of a resolution or positive outcome, then we are likely to get just that – a stuck feeling. An attitude of hopefulness combined with an openness to the possibility of positive change is more likely to produce desired progress.

As I remain with the felt sense of not feeling appreciated, deeper meanings come into sharper focus. I begin to notice that what really bothers me is that when I express my vulnerable feelings, I do not experience them being received sensitively – then I feel hurt. That says it better. That is a deeper level of what I'm feeling (hurt) and what it is about (not feeling appreciated). I feel more release in my body as I sense my genuine feeling of hurt. And as I begin to understand the wisdom it reflects, I feel even better. My chest relaxes.

Instead of feeling totally powerless and at the mercy of the other person's actions, I now have a clearer understanding of my reactions and my deeper need for contact that is not being met. I still feel hurt to realize that my feelings are not being sensitively received, but it now has a changed quality to it – a different edge. It has somehow become manageable and easier to accept. There is a curious richness to the feeling; I no longer have an aversion to feeling hurt. It is okay to feel it. As I become more friendly with the hurt, that too begins to pass and I feel a new sense of peace inside myself. And, curiously, I feel more caring toward my friend.

Focusing is not an analytical process. Positive changes happen through an ability to remain with present feelings, rather than analyze past causes. If I were strictly a Freudian or psychoanalytically oriented therapist, I would probably examine my observation that my feelings are not being sensitively received. I would look to the past for my present feeling of being misunderstood. I would re-examine significant earlier times when I felt people were being insensitive to me. I would especially explore the childhood relationship with my parents and how previous feelings of rejection might be unrealistically distorting how I am perceiving my present relationship.

Sometimes these past patterns are, indeed, influencing the present situation. A Focusing session (whether self-led, or facilitated by a therapist or guide) will allow for the possibility of relevant memories to arise. In my own therapy practice, I notice that exploring past experiences is often especially illuminating for people who have not spent much time recognizing the past roots of present discontents.

Difficulties can arise, however, when the past is elevated to a supreme position in the therapy process, which explains why psychoanalysis traditionally takes many years. We can always discover prior experiences that resemble our current ones, but if we reduce *all* of our present discomfort to past causes, then we may develop the unfortunate habit of missing the life we are currently living. We can easily become lost in endless labyrinths of past situations and rehash old feelings without making substantial progress.

Focusing is present oriented. We do not *try* to make connections with the past. If old memories or relevant associations happen to arise, they are embraced within the context of the present. They are explored or re-experienced with an intention to help us better understand our present behavior and remove obstacles to experiencing greater aliveness, spontaneity, and harmony with ourselves and others.

As my Focusing session proceeds, I may spontaneously recall times in the past when my feelings were not understood or appreciated. But the main issue I am now dealing with is that I do not feel sensitively received by *this* particular individual. I have already felt a shift in perspective and my body has released some tension that was holding the problem in place. I check to see if I want to do more Focusing, or if this feels like a good place to rest for now. I know that if I take on too much, I can lose some of the gains I've already made.

I listen to my body sense. Do I feel complete or does this issue need more attention right now? I wait. I feel complete for now. I take some time to be with how I feel now. I sense a fresh perspective and new insight regarding an issue I had not been able to resolve through mental analysis or by talking to well-meaning friends. Most importantly, I feel a new sense of openness and well-being within my body. I can breathe a little more deeply. I feel more alive. I have a new sense of hope about this issue and my life in general as I experience a small, yet significant step forward.

Focusing provides no miracle cures or instant answers to difficult issues we've been struggling with for a long time. But I know that Focusing has led me to take an important step that can never be lost. The next time I'm ready to Focus, I'll be that much further along.

The growth process is never-ending. We never become a 'finished' product. Life can be felt and lived as a process of continual change and growth. But this can happen only if we allow it to take its natural course without resisting the depths of its hurts, the heights of its joyful moments, and the breadth of its ordinariness – learning to live day to day grounded in the simple bodily felt awareness that Focusing encourages.

The next time I am ready to Focus, a variety of options may arise that will further change the nature of my friendship. It is impossible to know, merely by thinking about it right now, what new discoveries might arise out of my bodily felt process. Perhaps, while Focusing, I will feel a need to communicate to her that I am not feeling sensitively received and notice if anything changes by virtue of expressing my concern. Or, a positive direction may be the discovery that I need to give up my attempt to get this from her. I may realize that I need to take a step back from the relationship because it will not provide what I need. Or, maybe I will realize that I am not getting what I want because I am demanding too much; if I can accept her more and ask for less, then she may feel more free to give me what I want.

Any of these alternatives, or a totally unpredictable one, is possible. In any case, the one that feels 'right' for *me* will encourage further progress in my personal and interpersonal life. As a result, the friendship will never be exactly the same again. *I* will never be exactly the same. If I have the courage to truly confront the issues at hand and act in ways harmonious with my felt experience, then whatever happens will be a positive outcome. Whether a deeper closeness develops or I am freed to pursue other friendships, a sense of resolution will emerge as I continue to consult with my ongoing felt experience.

CONCLUSION

Focusing taps a core creative process existing in each of us. As such, many people, at least at times, have touched upon this rich vein of bodily felt knowing within themselves. For them, Focusing can provide a fine tuning of an innate capacity.

Once Focusing is sufficiently mastered, it may be used as a self-help therapy. Or it may be even more productively used in pairs (whether Focusing by yourself or with another person, the Appendix offers helpful guidelines). Being led through the process by a skilled guide – whether a therapist, spouse, or friend – we can receive useful assistance through his or her role of asking facilitating questions and providing support through a quality of empathy and caring. Through its gentle, allowing manner, Focusing can provide a safe context through which vulnerably to share what is happening in our inner world.

CHAPTER 6
The Focusing steps

Focusing involves the use of open-ended questions[1] designed to invite our experiential process to become more fully accessible to awareness. Gendlin originally used the term 'experiential therapy' to refer to the fact that the client's felt experience deserves primary attention, rather than the therapist's interpretations, or our own mental efforts to figure out solutions. As we approach presently felt experience in an honest, direct, and friendly way, then issues, feelings, and meanings that may be unclear are given an opportunity to come into sharper focus. The following are the Focusing steps, as we teach them,[2] along with commentaries to clarify the purpose of each phase of the process. These steps may be used by yourself or, often more effectively, with the assistance of a guide (the Appendix contains a condensed version of these steps for easier reference).

PREPARATION

Take some time to relax within yourself . . . (pause). Allow your attention to settle into your body, noticing how you feel inside . . . (pause at least one minute).

We often come to Focusing from the busyness of our day. This preparatory step provides us an opportunity to relax. It gives us time to settle into the present moment and allows calming of the rampant chatter that our minds often engage in. Directing our attention inside the body is one of the most effective ways to quiet distracting thoughts. In fact, research has shown that those people who engage in the calming practice of meditation find it easier to Focus (Weiss, 1978; Amodeo, 1981a).

Although many people naturally close their eyes while Focusing, you may wish to keep them open, gently cast downwards about three feet ahead of you. Letting your eyes remain open is sometimes helpful in maintaining a calm alertness, particularly if you tend to become sleepy or lethargic when they are closed. Experimentation will help you discover the approach that works best for you.

STEP 1 CLEARING A SPACE BY TAKING AN INVENTORY

(a) **Allowing your attention to remain inside your body, notice if there's anything going on in your life that's getting in the way of feeling really good right now (pause . . . wait for response).**

The purpose of step 1(a) is to become aware of all the issues that are inhibiting your *present* sense of well-being. The word 'present' is emphasized because many times we carry around a long list of problems or complaints. However, in any given moment we may be surprised to discover that what we *think* are problematic issues are not actually *felt* to be difficult when we consult our body's version of what is happening in our lives. In other words, we are often habitually weighed down by a number of assumed problems that we carry around in our minds. On the other hand, concerns may arise that surprise us, whether they are new issues or 'golden oldies' that continue to haunt us.

This step also allows us to clear the clutter in our minds by getting an organized sense of our current life issues, or condensing a seemingly large number of present concerns into a more manageable set of issues. We may be somewhat relieved to discover that what seemed like two or three separate issues are actually components of a larger one. For example, an issue about our job and the concern that our partner has been distant lately may both be part of a larger concern about a lack of nurturing contact in our lives.

We may at times feel a vague discontent without being able to identify any specific issue to which it relates. It may take us a minute or more to notice if anything identifiable emerges that connects with our unclear feeling. Ascertaining these concerns is an important step toward resolving them. If, however, we are unable to identify a specific issue, then we can simply allow our vague discomfort or uneasiness to be there without the effort to understand it immediately.

(b) Just notice whatever issue or concern arose for you and see if you can set it aside for now . . . (pause until you get a feeling for putting it aside or setting it down).

Once we come to fully acknowledge a presently felt concern, we allow ourselves a bit of distance from it by setting it aside. Putting issues aside is like setting down a bulky load of groceries when we return from shopping. Once we put them down, then we can look inside and sort through them as we wish. Putting issues aside enables us to be with them from a different perspective – one that is less overwhelmed by heavy concerns. Being exclusively identified with a problem means that we are being dominated or controlled by it. But if we can find a comfortable distance from an important matter or allow some space to surround an issue, then we can work with it more effectively. Zen Master Shunryu Suzuki uses an apt analogy when he says. 'To give your sheep or cow a large, spacious meadow is the way to control him.'[3] Similarly, the best way to deal with our thoughts and emotions is to let them be as they are and develop a caring relationship with them.

Finding the right distance between yourself and relevant concerns is helpful when dealing with issues that are particularly difficult, or ones that have been ignored for a long time. For example, if you are feeling irritated with your spouse you may get bogged down with continually negative thoughts about him or her, as well as feel burdened by the weight of a general cynicism toward life. Instead of being dominated by all this, you can take some time to be with how you feel in relation to the problem. Experiencing some space around a burdensome issue, you may begin to develop a sense of yourself being *with* the issue rather than *being* the issue.

Faced with a particularly scary or difficult concern, you may include the optional step of asking yourself, 'Can I feel a basic sense of "okayness" as I allow this problem to be there next to me?' If you cannot feel this after a few minutes, that's okay too.

Then proceed to Step 2 and skip (c). An issue that cannot be set aside is often in need of immediate attention.

(c) **Is there anything else going on in your life that's getting between you and feeling good right now?** (Wait for an inner response.)

(d) **Just notice whatever came up for you. Can you put that aside for now?**

(e) **As you continue to allow your attention to rest inside your body, notice if there's anything else getting in the way of feeling good right now.**

(Continue in this way, using sequence (d) and (e) until no further issues arise.)

(f) **Is there anything else in your life right now that is not a problem, but that would like attention?** (If so, set that aside as well.)

The practice of Focusing is not restricted to an exploration of problems or painful issues, although these are often the ones requiring immediate attention. You may also wish to explore new life directions or Focus on something you feel good about in order to enjoy new understandings that can help your life move in a positive direction. One individual, for example, wanted to explore ways to spend more meaningful time with her children. This was not a pressing problem, but she sensed that a deeper fulfillment awaited her in this regard.

Sometimes when Focusing, no difficulties arise. In addition, there may be no positive concerns wanting attention. If this occurs, you may allow yourself to relish the pleasant, open feeling as presently felt within yourself. Appreciating your sense of organismic well-being, you may allow it to expand more and more if it wishes to. At some point during such a 'meditative' period, an issue may arise that you feel inclined to Focus upon. If not, you can continue to enjoy your good feeling for as long as you like.

STEP 2 SENSING WHICH ONE WANTS ATTENTION RIGHT NOW

(a) **Of all these issues that came up for you, which one stands out the most? Which one wants attention right now?**

This simple step merely identifies the issue that you feel most drawn toward in a 'felt' way. Does one of them feel the most pressing or the heaviest? Does one have more pressure behind it or tension in it? Does one stand out the most or call for your attention in some way? Trust what comes, even if you are surprised.

Do not be so concerned if there is difficulty discerning the issue that is most in need of attention. On a deeper level, all life issues interconnect; the most vital one may be encountered through the doorway of a related concern.

It is important to notice whenever you are censoring yourself while sensing the issues most in need of attention, as by saying, 'I really shouldn't be bothered by this insignificant little concern.' Judging, minimizing, or invalidating your genuinely felt experience is a sure way to keep yourself stuck and unhappy. Whatever is felt as a concern for you needs to be taken seriously because it is important to *you*. And seemingly small matters are often doorways to more consequential ones. For example, one woman in our Focusing group was bothered by the fact that her next-door neighbor was forgetting to feed his pet rabbit. Although she thought this was a silly issue at first, she could not deny the fact that it was bothering her. Focusing upon it, she realized its significance as she began to get in touch with feelings of being emotionally undernourished in her own life. This important recognition led to a new positive direction for this individual.

STEP 3 IS IT OKAY TO BE WITH THIS?

(a) Is it okay to be with this for awhile? Just check to see if your body says 'yes' or 'no'. (Pause . . . if the answer is yes, go to Step 4(a).)

(b) If it's not okay, is it at least okay to be with how scary or difficult it is to get in touch with this right now? (If yes, notice how your body feels about this, then go to Step 4; if it's still not okay, then choose another issue that is okay to be with.)

Focusing is a gentle process. You choose your own pace. There is never a suggestion to explore an issue if you are not ready or willing to do so. In fact, any kind of force or pressure tends to interfere with the natural pace of Focusing. Rather than aggressively pushing yourself past barriers, you are invited to experience the barrier itself. The effort to press beyond an impasse often involves a kind of drivenness that will make you even more anxious, upset, or stuck.

Step 3 is a built-in safeguard that can be used throughout the Focusing process. It supports you to move very gently toward the real issues, feelings, and meanings that are happening in your life. If, at any time, it is not okay to be with a particular issue or feeling, then take a safe step back, gently allowing yourself to be with how scary or painful it is to Focus on what is there for you right now.

If you reach a difficult juncture, your Focusing process may be served by imagining yourself putting your arm around the painful issue or frightening feeling, or, you may use the image of putting your arm around yourself, as you would with a hurting child. Such images convey the attitude that is most helpful to increasingly embody during Focusing: caring, friendliness, and compassion toward all that you are. Being gentle and loving toward the tight, difficult areas within yourself can often provide the warmth necessary to slowly melt a hard, constricted area that you have been stuck with, or have been struggling to avoid. You may then be surprised to find yourself more open to hurt, lonely, or scared feelings within yourself, as well as more willing to explore the feelings and meanings contained in important life issues that you have bypassed or minimized.

Proceeding to explore in a caring manner whatever arises while Focusing often leads to a glad willingness to open to felt experience, even if it means facing pain or occasional tears. This willingness, however, may take time and practice. Small successes may gradually empower you to move ahead courageously.

If you feel too uncomfortable at the present time to Focus upon a particular concern, that is all right. You may then choose another issue that you feel more comfortable being with. Or, you may opt to allow yourself to stop for now.

STEP 4 ALLOWING A FELT SENSE TO FORM

(a) 'How does this whole issue or situation feel inside your body right now?' . . . (pause) [If not much comes, ask the following questions in order to invite your felt sense to come into clearer focus]:
(b) 'Where in your body do you feel it?' . . . (pause)
(c) 'What does it feel like?' . . . (pause)
(d) Take some time to fully sense this whole issue or situation inside of you, apart from your thoughts about it.

As discussed earlier, Focusing is based upon bodily felt experiencing. This stage helps you deepen into how your body is carrying the issues that may normally be considered only by your rational mind. Step 4(b) encourages you to sense the bodily location of the issue at hand. Do you feel it mainly in your stomach or chest or throat? Or do you experience it as a generalized sense throughout your entire body?

We tend to feel things in the upper part of our bodies. That is where our heart, stomach, and other inner organs reside; that is where we are most prone to experience feelings such as fear or hurt. Body armor often develops as an attempt to shield our vulnerable areas from imagined or real threats from other people or life circumstances. Our bodies contract and tighten in order to protect these tender places.

Step 4(c) invites you to sense the quality of how an issue feels inside you. Does it feel heavy, tense, fluttery, light, tingling, cold, hot, or constricted? Or are you aware of some other felt quality?

Whatever comes, we can take some time to sense it inside us, without the usual efforts to analyze, control, or 'figure it out.' Psychologists use the term 'intellectualizing' to describe how we often use thoughts and ideas to defend ourselves from our true feelings. The inability or unwillingness to allow awareness to filter down into our bodily felt experiencing is one of the most commonly encountered obstacles to Focusing. With practice, perseverance, and, perhaps, the help of a skilled facilitator, even those who find it enormously difficult to sense inside their bodies can, in time, gradually open to this new dimension of experiencing.

When dealing with difficult issues, Step 4 allows us to gently hold what we usually reject or avoid. Sometimes painful feelings arise at this juncture. If we allow the pain or fear to be there, rather than try to avoid it, then these feelings have a chance to release themselves. If something comes that is especially difficult, then, again, the image of gently and caringly holding it, like a baby, can often help us be with this feeling in a way that can lead to positive changes.[4]

It is not useful to *expect* painful feelings to come; they may or may not arise. Focusing can lead to many surprises, including unexpected breakthroughs. But if pain, fear, or an unpleasant feeling does come, it is helpful to allow yourself to be with it in a friendly way, rather than becoming critical of yourself for having such a feeling.

The fastest way to grow is through accepting the experiences we normally resist, such as our hurt and pain. Fighting our feelings only leads to more pain and frustration. Holding back our tears, for example, actually hurts more than allowing ourselves to cry. As we open to our natural feelings, we begin to feel better. Touching our experience more deeply and directly, inner tensions can find a welcome release. As a result, we feel stronger, increasingly confident, and more at peace with ourselves. We know ourselves more fully. We are more in touch with ourselves. As a result, our relationships have a greater chance of becoming rich sources of nourishment, joy, and love.

STEP 5 ALLOWING THE FELT SENSE TO EXPRESS ITSELF

(a) Now, staying with how your body feels about the whole issue or situation, allow a word, phrase, or image (etc.) to come that expresses how your body feels . . .

(b) Just let yourself be with how you're feeling that whole sense of – (whatever word, phrase, or image, etc., came up) . . . Then, if anything more wants to come to you as you stay with that, allow it to come.

(Continue in this way, using Step (b) to be with each new thing as it may arise, whether a word, phrase, image, memory, or felt meaning. If something particularly painful or difficult emerges, see if you can be with it in a friendly, caring way.)

(After several cycles, when you sense that there has been some release, you can ask:)

(c) Does that feel complete for now, or is there something that would like more attention? (If you feel complete, go to Step 6; if not, return to (c).)

Step 5 requires skill and imagination in terms of learning the art of asking the right questions. While Step 4 of Focusing involves contacting the felt sense, Step 5 (a) invites our felt sense to speak through a variety of possible expressions. This may be in the form of a word, phrase, or image. In addition, sometimes a memory or sense of meaning will arise that expresses something significant in relation to how we deeply feel. As we remain with how these expressions feel inside us, we may experience a release of tensions or a 'felt shift.' For example, we may be experiencing a tightness in the throat that relates to our partner's desire to spend time with other people. As we open to how this feels inside us, a word such as 'shaky' may come. This word resonates with how we are inwardly sensing this issue. Or a phrase may arise such as 'shaky trust,' which expresses something significant about how we are experiencing her wish to be with others. Or an image of standing alone may spontaneously appear. Or, rather than a word, phrase, or image that connects with our felt sense, we may notice a memory or a sense of meaning that spontaneously arises. These are more likely to occur in the next phase (step 5(b)), after we have spent some time Focusing. However, they may also appear here. For instance, we may notice a memory of being abandoned by a parent or friend. Or a sense of meaning related to our tight throat may emerge, such as, 'I'm holding back telling her how I feel because I'm afraid she might leave me.'

Each of the above expressions are meaningful communications from our bodily felt sense. Whichever one happens to come, we are then able to experience a more substantial sense of our fluid, elusive experiential process. As our inner experience reveals itself in this manner, we gradually move toward a greater sense of relief and peace of mind in relation to our troublesome concern.

Step 5 (b) invites us to continue being aware of how our body is experiencing each new item that arises, be it a fresh image, word, phrase, feeling, memory, or sense of meaning. Being with this in a friendly caring manner enables underlying feelings and meanings to spontaneously rise to the surface of awareness. It is as if layers of the onion were beginning to peel away, enabling us to discover what lies at our depths.

An example may help clarify the recycling aspect of Step 5(b). Amy was Focusing on her relationship with Jeff. She felt a sense of discouragement about the way they related. She first noticed a heavy feeling in her chest. She sat quietly with this bodily felt sense, and noticed if anything more wanted to emerge. Any number of possibilities existed. As her attention remained with the heavy feeling in her chest, the word 'hopeless' arose. She then stayed with this sense of hopelessness and noticed if anything else wished to arise. She waited. After several minutes she saw an image of land caving in. Being with the *feeling* of this image, she realized how she kept giving in to Jeff. 'I'm not standing up for myself by saying how I feel!' This was an important part of the meaning contained in the feeling. In effect, it reflected an inclination to give up on herself and on being happy in the relationship. Amy then stayed aware of how her body was experiencing this whole sense of not standing up for herself. After waiting a few minutes, she soon noticed some fluttering in her stomach. Then it came to her – 'I'm angry!' She soon felt a little better as she took some time to sense the anger. As she opened to the feeling of anger, she realized that she needed to stand up for herself more – to say 'No.' This was the wisdom contained in the anger. Continuing to Focus on the anger, she then realized that she felt left out whenever Jeff wanted to visit other friends. As she took several minutes to be friendly toward this feeling of being left out, she noticed sadness. 'I want to feel closer to Jeff. I'm missing that.' As she stayed with her bodily experience of all this, she felt an impulse to tell Jeff how much he meant to her and that she would like to spend more time with him. Feeling a sigh of relief, she realized the deeper feelings that had been underlying her initial feeling of discouragement.

The key to Step 5(c) is to simply be with our bodily felt experience of each successive word, image, feeling, or meaning that arises. And as we remain with how *that* feels we may notice something new that will then become the next object of our sustained attention. A common temptation during this gradual process is to resort to our familiar insights, judgments, and mental interpretations. Although our minds have been well-trained to jump in and try to settle the matter, they are not well-equipped to tap the deeper knowing that resides in the very depths of our being. As we Focus, we can practice noticing each of these mental diversions as they happen to arise, and then gently return to felt experience.

It is during Step 5(b) that a felt shift is most likely to happen. This may come about in two possible ways. In one instance, we feel a release by simply being open to a previously scary or difficult feeling. By sitting with our anger, opening to our fear, or holding our hurt, these feelings may gradually pass if we can give them adequate time and attention. We can feel surprisingly better, knowing what our real feelings are, and allowing them simply to be.

We may also enjoy a feeling of release through gaining a sense of meaning regarding a particular feeling or set of feelings. A 'felt meaning' in the previous example came when Amy realized that she was not standing up for herself. An additional felt meaning, leading to an even more distinctly felt shift, was realizing how much she really liked and wanted to be with Jeff, though she had not expressed that. Understanding the wisdom contained within our feelings – not merely in a mental way, but, more importantly, in a *felt* way, leads to fresh perspectives and an open, spacious feeling that accompanies the release of bodily held tensions.

There may be times during Focusing when we are uncertain regarding whether an arising thought reflects a felt meaning or is merely an idea disconnected from our feelings. If this uncertainty occurs, we may check it out by going inside ourselves and noticing whether the thought connects with our bodily sense of the issue at hand. Thoughts are not antithetical to Focusing, although our minds have tried to be in control for so long that we often need to correct the matter by de-emphasizing them. Focusing is an integrated approach that unites body and mind, thinking and feeling, cognition and intuition. Thoughts can be useful when connected to felt experience.

You may Focus until you arrive at a natural resting place. Again, consult your body. It knows whether you feel complete or if you need to spend more time with some issue.

OPTIONAL STEP 5(e). 'ASKING'

(You may use this step if you seem to be stuck.)

1. Exploratory questions:

   –Staying with how your body feels about the whole issue or situation, notice if you get any sense of what that's about.

   –What's the main thing about all this that's really getting to you?

   –What's the worst (or best) thing about it?

   –What is it about this whole issue you're dealing with that has you feeling so – (Whatever word or phrase that may have arisen that matches your feelings)?

2 Forward moving questions:

   –Do you have a sense of what direction would feel like a small step forward with all this?

   –What direction would feel like a breath of fresh air?

   –What needs to happen in order for you to feel better about the whole situation? . . . Is anything getting in the way of that happening?

Optional Step 5(e) is helpful when we need a little encouragement. Sometimes we will feel stuck, like a record that keeps skipping. If we can simply take one small step on to the next groove, we may move ahead more smoothly. It is best not to expect huge shifts as if anticipating orchestra cymbals clashing in the background. It is often the small, subtle shifts that steadily lead to major positive changes. Growing up in our present culture, we are accustomed to instant results, as when we turn on the television to be instantly entertained. Unproductive patterns that we have learned over time take time to unlearn. We may guarantee failure by setting our goals too high. Since we cannot possibly achieve them, we give up – perhaps re-convincing ourselves that we are stupid or beyond help.

The 'exploratory questions' are designed to make specific inquiries of your felt experience in order to coax it into speaking more clearly to you. They are especially geared toward eliciting a hidden dimension of felt meaning, which is often helpful when your Focusing process slows or is stuck. These questions may also assist you to connect your bodily felt sense with a life issue you are working with. For example, if you are exploring an issue about work and are experiencing a heaviness in your chest that is best expressed by the word 'frustrated,' you can ask yourself, 'what is it about work that feels so frustrating?' Or, you may ask, 'what's the most frustrating thing about it?' Perhaps it has to do with the long hours, or an unsupportive boss, or a lack of meaning in your job.

'Forward moving' questions may be useful to encourage you to sense the direction in which your process would like to move in order to begin resolving itself. Such questions may help you tap a natural inner wisdom or basic organismic intelligence that knows the direction in which your life needs to move. Perhaps, for instance, you can sense that communicating your real feelings would lead to a welcome release. Or you may sense that a step forward would be to open yourself to other people instead of depending so much on your partner to meet all your needs. *You* know better than anyone else how you are experiencing life, as well as the unique steps forward that are appropriate for you. Learn to trust what comes. If a new feeling, meaning, or direction occurs as you ask a 'forward moving' question, take some time to be with how your body is experiencing that. You may then continue to allow your process to unfold in this manner. Returning to Step 5(b) may then be helpful in facilitating your ongoing Focusing process.

The sequence involved in Step 5 may be seen as a process of 'unlayering.' As one layer of a vaguely felt concern rises to awareness, take some time to be with the feelings and meanings contained in that layer of experience. Then, as additional elements spontaneously come to awareness, simply open to the bodily felt experience of each of these. As this process continues, deeper layers of what is true for you will emerge into conscious awareness. As a result, you are likely to gradually enjoy the satisfaction of being more intimately connected with yourself.

STEP 6 ALLOWING YOURSELF TO BE

Just allow yourself to be with how you feel inside right now, perhaps with a sense of appreciation or gratitude for whatever steps you may have taken.

Instead of brusquely ending a session, this simple step encourages you to take some time to be with a new sense of openness that may have resulted from Focusing. You may feel what it is like to be *you* in this new way. You may also take time enjoying a sense of appreciation for yourself or toward life in general. Personal growth seems to accelerate as we learn to embody an attitude of self-appreciation and a sense of gratitude for small, yet significant steps forward.

As you conclude a Focusing session, you may best preserve whatever gains you have made by avoiding the temptation to once again figure things out with your rational mind, or ponder what happened while Focusing. Returning to a problem-solving or thinking mode means returning to the controlling, analytical mind that was suspended as you began to Focus. At a later time, you may wish to Focus further on a particular concern, or on some new aspect of that concern.

It may be encouraging to realize that if you have been Focusing properly, an issue will rarely be felt in exactly the same way as before. Issues tend to recur when we have neglected to deal with them in an effective, experiential way. Although the same or similar concerns may later arise, they will tend to be experienced in a slightly different (if not transformed) way.

This concluding step of allowing ourselves to simply *be* also enables us to make a smoother transition back to our lives in the world. We may, perhaps, notice a new, relaxed, spacious feeling as we complete a Focusing session and begin to engage in new activities. Whether we were gifted with a deeply felt release, fresh insights, or only minor progress (or none at all for a particular Focusing session), we can take some time to appreciate ourselves for attending to our lives in this honest, open way.

CHAPTER 7
Replacing the inner critic with an inner caretaker

The Focusing process involves the simple capacity to be with our felt experience. As we have seen, this natural ability is often lost or obscured during the process of socialization. Focusing can initially appear to be puzzling when feelings have been denied or minimized for a long time. Some of the difficulty may result from the tendency to separate those feelings deemed acceptable from those that are not. This censoring of experience dilutes the potential effectiveness of contacting raw experience unblemished by our preferences or evaluations.

Whether or not we have ready access to feelings, Focusing can be more effective if we notice the interfering effects of a phenomenon that we will refer to as the 'inner critic.' This term symbolizes a deeply ingrained tendency to be critical of ourselves and others. This judgmental inclination of mind cues us as to what is supposedly 'right and wrong,' 'good and bad,' or 'appropriate and inappropriate.' This phenomenon may manifest as a pervasive background feeling that dampens our energies and unknowingly influences our behavior. At times we may more accurately identify this background feeling as an 'inner cynic' that negatively pervades our lives and activities, discouraging us from making the effort to change and grow. This disempowering inner cynic holds us back, keeping us from actualizing our full potential, often through deflating statements such as, 'You can never be happy,' 'Don't bother trying,' and 'You'll never make it!'

If the inner critic is particularly harsh, or if our inner cynic has been in control for a long time, we may benefit by first exploring this tendency itself prior to Focusing. Access to our real feelings is severely hindered if we instantly invalidate certain unwanted emotions such as hurt or anger, or if we remain anxiously watchful over ourselves to insure that our feelings and actions will be acceptable in the eyes of others. Being quick to cut ourselves off from experience deemed inappropriate or too risky, we fail to give our feelings the impartial hearing they need.

The inner critic is usually born out of past rejections and critical statements by others that we have learned to direct internally toward ourselves. For example, one client was often chastised as a child for wanting contact with his distracted and unavailable parents. He was frequently told, 'You're such a chatter-box!' and 'children should be seen and not heard!' As a result, he learned to avoid parental criticism by silently saying to himself, 'shut up' and 'you're talking too much.' As a sensitive child who wanted to avoid these painful attacks and invalidating judgments, he began to judge and evaluate himself in order to gain approval or at least avoid the hurtful disapproval of others.

Behaviors and feelings that are punished or discouraged by parents, teachers, or other elders, or those that are ridiculed by peers, are scrupulously avoided through the controlling restraint of the inner critic. The unconscious decision that is made in order to adopt this system of self-repression is that there is something terribly wrong with us. We learn not only to distrust ourselves to express how we feel, but soon discover that it is not even safe to trust our bodily felt experience or needs themselves, since doing so repeatedly leads to reproach or invalidation.

Upon this foundation of self-mistrust we begin operating from barely audible thoughts such as, 'If I want to be accepted and loved, I'd better do and say what people want;' or, 'If I just do better (according to others' standards or ones we learn from them), then I'll be accepted and secure.' Learning to criticize and judge ourselves in ways designed to win approval, we may begin to experience who we are in the harsh light of this inner critic. Pushing ourselves to meet parental demands or societal expectations, we increasingly identify with socially conditioned experience that further and further removes us from our genuine, organismically felt experience.

By learning to recognize the various guises of the inner critic, you can move toward reaffirming your underlying felt experience. Since the particular criticisms and judgments to which we are subject are unique for each of us, it is up to you to become familiar with the particular way in which this inner critic influences you. It is only through learning to discriminate the voice or 'feeling' of the critic as it arises within that you will overcome this particularly obstinate hindrance to Focusing.

One way that the inner critic often manifests in our culture is through the injunction that we should not feel angry or sad. For instance, one client was repeatedly told each time he tried to express anger that he was a 'bad boy' and that he would 'go to hell for talking like that.' Similarly, if we are feeling sad or hurt, we may be accustomed to hearing others invalidate this feeling through statements such as 'Cheer up, it'll be okay,' or 'Don't cry, it's not that bad.' Such refrains heard over and over (perhaps accompanied by punishment as a child, or threatening statements such as 'only babies cry,' or 'I'll give you something to cry about!'), may continue to haunt us in our adult lives, returning in some subtle way whenever we feel strong emotions. For instance, if we are grieving the loss of a relationship, we may be angry with ourselves for not feeling resolved about it: 'What's wrong with me? I should be over this by now.' Unfortunately, as a result of trying to get rid of the grief, we deny the natural process that would enable it to pass, thus perpetuating it. Focusing on this experience of anger toward ourselves, we may recognize that this feeling is being generated by our inner critic. Observing this, we may disengage from our self-criticism and allow ourselves to 'free fall,' as it were, into our more deeply felt experience.

In addition to judging feelings as acceptable or unacceptable, the inner critic may also tell us how to behave. For example, while Focusing, it may occur to you that a positive step forward would be to express that you feel angry or hurt in relation to a friend. Although this action may appear as a fresh alternative that feels 'right' during an illumined moment of being with felt experience, you may soon lose interest in putting this step into practice, or even abandon it altogether as a result of the critic's inhibiting logic. You may then wonder if Focusing really works since you rarely act on your new insights. Or you may conclude that you are lazy or cowardly (additional critical judgments) for not actualizing your insights gained in Focusing.

What may be occurring in such instances where you fail to act on your newly felt wisdom is that the subtly convincing and tenacious inner critic has returned. For example, you may be seduced once again by the idea (solidified over the years) that you do not have the right to express how you feel because it might upset the other person. While some genuine caring may be present here, the deeper concern often consists of what others may think of you, or the possible negative consequences of overstepping conventional social boundaries. Your inner critic might promptly react by keeping you from doing or saying anything that is socially taboo, exerting whatever control is necessary to keep you in line.

One way to begin discerning the influence of the critic is to notice when you use obligatory words such as 'should,' 'ought,' 'must,' 'have to,' or 'can't.' Observing yourself driven by a 'should,' it would be wise to pause for a few moments to discriminate between ideas about how you 'should' feel and behave from what you actually feel and want. As you consistently do this, you may grow to act with greater freedom and self-determination. Releasing yourself from enslavement to the socially conditioned critic, you will find yourself moving from a stance of powerlessness and obligation to one of empowerment and enthusiasm for acting from your own choices and preferences.

Another common manner in which the critic manifests is by making comparisons between ourselves and others. For example, we may find ourselves checking whether we measure up in appearance, expressiveness, wardrobe, or financial and professional status. The tendency to compare ourselves to others may also obstruct us in the first Focusing step of 'Clearing a Space.' We may find it difficult to honor genuine issues because they are quickly judged to be 'too trivial' compared to the problems of others. Reluctant to acknowledge a life issue because we imagine it to be insignificant or embarrassing, the critical mind may quickly banish this issue from awareness before we ever have a chance to glimpse it clearly.

Through secretly driving you or subtly invalidating you, the critic makes self-actualization difficult, if not impossible. Human beings can only grow by opening to genuinely felt experience. If this fault-finding tendency exerts a pressure that obscures your felt experience, then you are continually turning away from the very door you must enter in order to enjoy personal growth and meaning in your relationships. Standing up to the critic and re-owning the power that was surrendered when you succumbed to its tyrannical influence is an important step toward re-owning your life. In order to disentangle yourself from the noxious influences of the critic, you must begin to identify yourself as separate from its nagging voice and experience yourself as the one who is being nagged at. As you sense some distance from it, you may ask, 'How does it feel to hear that voice, constantly harassing or chastising me?' Perhaps you feel beaten down, tired, or worn out. Hopefully, as you continue to sense this oppressive phenomenon inside yourself, you will begin to feel a spark of healthy anger – the inner child yearning to break free of that tyrannical voice. Honoring the anger and allowing a resounding 'NO' to spring forth, you may begin to re-own the autonomy and power that was relinquished to the critic during the process of conforming to social norms.

It is often helpful at this point to express anger or take a firm stand against those who taught us to criticize ourselves. While we are not suggesting that it is always wise to do this in a literal way, it can be surprisingly liberating to at least do so in your imagination. There can be great benefit in freely voicing the anger we would have expressed had we been allowed to do so as children. Allowing ourselves to now feel this healthy impulse to stand up for ourselves, we may begin to live more comfortably with our emotions as we no longer succumb to the tendency to stifle our feelings; refusing to take orders from the critic, we restore the basic integrity of who we are.

One group participant, for instance, was troubled by a hollow feeling in his stomach, which was related to worrying about his competence as a physician and as a father. Through some assistance, he recognized that this feeling was being generated by years of taking orders from his harsh inner critic. Experiencing shame for not living up to the 'super-doctor' ideals that he was taught in medical school, as well as feeling guilty for not being the constantly generous father he thought he should be, he began feeling relief as he gained some distance from this critical voice. Proceeding to have a dialogue with this inner critic, he told it to leave him alone and to accept the fact that he is fallible and human. This led to some healing tears as he affirmed himself as a human being with both strengths and limitations.

Once a clear boundary has been established between the critic and your underlying experiential process, you may gradually begin to make friends with the critic. This is a vital part of the process of learning compassion for all aspects of yourself, including the part that is inclined to push and judge you. Allowing time to respectfully relate to the critic whenever you notice it intruding upon you, you may discover what it really needs in order to leave you alone. For example, if the critic is concerned that you might become destitute, you can reassure it that you will do everything you can to forestall such an outcome.

Although its normal manner of functioning is usually harmful, the critic's judgments may contain elements of wisdom. For example, there may be legitimate concerns about your survival (such as issues regarding money) or physical well-being (such as diet and exercise). Hearing the well-meaning aspect of the critic is often difficult because it is expressed in such a negative and threatening way. Discriminating the kernel of wisdom that may reside in critical messages often leads to a lessening of the inner critic's demands. Its function may then be replaced by the felt presence of a wise and caring being who grants us the freedom to deal with our lives in a more relaxed, unpressured way.

Once you have recognized the way your inner critic operates and have begun to deal effectively with it, you can begin to develop a wise 'inner caretaker' – a part of yourself that generously allows your experience to simply be as it is. This ability to take care of yourself involves a wisdom and skill vitally necessary in order to cultivate happiness and peace of mind, as well as to initiate and develop satisfying intimate relationships. This nurturing, caretaking part of you can then gradually replace the inner critic, and serve the critic's healthier purposes much more skillfully.

DEVELOPING AN INNER CARETAKER

Perhaps the most basic way to care for yourself is embodied in the very practice of Focusing as we have described it. The process of Focusing involves a shift from conditioned beliefs, unexamined assumptions, and comfortable habits to a radical validation of your felt experience. As you move in the direction of fully accepting your experience, whatever it may be, you simultaneously come to accept and love yourself as you are. By honoring a full range of feelings and hearing the wisdom they contain, you become better friends with yourself. By 'accepting' or 'honoring' feelings, we mean the ability to be open to the direct experience of such feelings – the capacity to tolerate without trying to diminish, exaggerate, or dismiss whatever happens to present itself in any given moment. This simple act of accepting a full range of feelings means gently opening to how your body is experiencing them, followed by a calm attentiveness to the intelligence implicit within them.

Allowing our organism to experience fully in this caring manner creates a climate in which difficulties are most likely to be resolved. Unproductive or self-defeating patterns change as we learn to fully embrace our felt experience; whatever pain we may be carrying in relation to stressful life situations can be released by learning to cherish ourselves as we open to the experience of our pain. For example, Greg was in extreme anguish when Joan left him after a three-year relationship. He entered therapy several weeks later to deal with his pain. He soon experienced welcome relief after he courageously opened to his sorrow. Feeling better, he stopped coming for a while. Then, two months later, he returned when his pain once again became overwhelming. During the time away from therapy, Greg followed the suggestion to take time to be with himself, and he avoided resorting to his familiar habits of drinking and overworking. As a result, he had begun to sense a deep ache in the pit of his stomach. Focusing on it in a therapy session, he became impatient when it failed to pass quickly. He then had an important realization when it was pointed out that he was bargaining with his feelings – that is, agreeing to feel them only if they agreed to depart rapidly. When they did not, Greg would become discouraged with Focusing and with himself. By recognizing his manipulative intention and the voice of his inner critic, something began to shift. He took a deep breath and allowed himself to surrender more deeply to the aching feeling in his stomach until *it* was ready to pass. As he courageously stayed with the bodily felt sense of aching, he began to sob heavily. Images from his childhood were emerging – a scene of being slapped by his unfeeling father, and vivid memories of being rejected by women as a young man. He discovered that these earlier episodes, deeply ingrained and largely forgotten, were the underlying roots of his present anguish in regard to Joan.

Continuing to Focus on the ache in his stomach, Greg observed an image of himself as a little boy desperately needing love and affection. When asked if he could caringly place his arm around that hurt little boy, he began to gently cry. Greg then saw the possibility of developing a nurturing relationship with that hurt little boy – that is, with the child within himself – instead of trying to get it exclusively from an external source. The discovery that he could be a caretaker for himself brought substantial relief and an unaccustomed feeling of satisfaction. Being with his hurt in such a tender, gentle way gave rise to a rich discovery that led to a new sense of connectedness with himself. Although more Focusing was needed to consolidate these gains, Greg learned, through his own experience, how it felt to be friendly toward feelings that he normally avoided.

Becoming friends with the full range of our feelings moves us in the direction of no longer being threatened by them. Knowing that we can be with our hurt or fear as we would be with the hurt or fear of a child, we learn to provide comfort, love, and nurturing to ourselves. We grow through the discovery that embracing feelings in a welcoming manner does not lead to some dreaded paralysis, but to just the opposite – a rich experience of wholeness and well-being.

Through befriending our inner world, we can breathe more deeply as we grow to trust that we can meet life events without bracing ourselves against our experience – without resisting life itself.

Learning to trust that you can take care of yourself means that you become your own best friend. Confident that you can gently hold your hurts and fears, you can relax with the self-assurance that you can face and learn from difficult experiences. Trusting your capacity to do this creates a firm foundation from which to confidently open to others. Without such self-trust, there is no safe place to return to if your attempts to reach out fail, as they sometimes do. In fact, trusting others may not be possible without some prior trust in your capacity to be with the full range of feelings that will inevitably arise as a result of your contact with people. Trusting that you can be a caretaker for these feelings provides the dependable, ever-present resource necessary to move toward the creation of lasting intimate bonds. We then have the strength and ability to be vulnerable with others because we know we can be with hurt and sadness if they happen to arise. Trusting ourselves to deal with these potential feelings also empowers us to take intelligent risks in relationships. If others fail to respond in a way we might like, then we may feel hurt for a while, but it is no longer such a big deal.

Befriending unpleasant feelings for a sufficient duration to experience a healing shift can act as a kind of inoculation against potential future emotional threats. Having fully confronted the bodily felt experience of hurt or fear, an inner channel opens that may then re-open more easily when we encounter similar feelings in the future. Of course, there may still be difficult or painful feelings to face; but, having effectively dealt with the pain even once can give us the confidence to again engage such feelings in a bodily felt way, hear the meanings they may convey, and re-discover a sense of peace within ourselves.

Entering a relationship with our guard lowered and our self-assurance heightened, we are more likely to connect intimately in the way we desire. In fact, if we enter relationships cautiously protecting our vulnerable soft spots, communications tend to be misunderstood and tensions may begin to accumulate. If we are tentative or guarded in our interactions, people often sense that we are holding something back. This can increase their discomfort or mistrust, and decrease the likelihood that they will be with us in the open intimate way we would like. In addition, the better we feel about ourselves, the easier it is to communicate with sensitivity and caring, rather than in a critical or blaming manner. Enjoying greater self-affirmation, we tend to respond less defensively to others' unkind words or actions. We can also hear people's negative feelings (such as anger or hurt) without reacting defensively. Until our inner caretaker is well developed, we will tend to hear others' expressions of feelings as criticism or pressure, instead of as their feelings.

Being able to take care of ourselves enables us to hear people's responses to us in a calmer, more realistic way. Positive reactions can then be received without exaggerating their significance. Negative expressions can be evaluated in relation to our own felt experience, without, on the one hand, immediately disagreeing or counter-attacking, or, on the other hand, feeling badly about ourselves, fearful that others' opinions or feelings may mean something awful about us. As we build a firm foundation of trust and positive regard for ourselves, we can hear feedback with an attitude of curiosity and an interest in our further growth. Then, instead of arousing our inner critic, input can be received within a context of self-affirmation as we appreciate our strengths and recognize our limitations. We are then well-situated to acknowledge others' feelings, and accept whatever feedback feels appropriate, while discarding the rest.

Caring for past hurts is another significant way to be a caretaker for ourselves. It is extremely difficult, if not impossible, to move toward a full-fledged current involvement while still encumbered with unresolved feelings from previous relationships. If we are carrying old hurts from past rejections, we are likely to be haunted by them as we verge on a closer intimate involvement in the present. Being a gentle caretaker for these past wounds, we become more available for involvement in a new relationship.

The direction that often emerges as a result of being caringly present to these past upsets is one of forgiving others for whatever pain they may have caused us (or seemed to cause us). By 'forgiveness,' we do not mean the conventional, polite act of pardoning others for offensive words or deeds. Mentally wishing or thinking forgiveness, or just saying the words, is vastly different from actually *feeling* forgiveness. Clients of ours, for example, sometimes wonder why a partner cannot simply 'forgive and forget' regarding some incident that may have happened long ago. The real experience of forgiveness cannot occur through a mental decision – it results from experiencing and being released from our resentments and the underlying pain and hurt. This requires a capacity to be with our feelings in an internally caring way – especially when the other person continues to be emotionally unavailable to work things through with us. The term 'resolution' or 'healing' may more aptly

describe the real intention behind the commonly misunderstood
term· 'forgiveness.'

Being able to forgive *ourselves* is another important way to
take care of ourselves. Being human, there are times when we
are bound to make mistakes or contribute to another person's
hurt. Rather than paralyzing ourselves through unproductive
self-condemnation, we can work toward satisfying relationships
by allowing ourselves to experience remorse, reflecting upon
important lessons, and opening in a fresh way to others.

Whether our inner caretaker chooses to Focus on past hurts
or present difficulties, the path toward a richer life does not
predominantly involve feeling 'happier' but, rather, feeling more.
This is especially true in the early stages of growth, when the
force of stored emotions may suddenly gush forth. But even the
most self-actualized individuals are prone to experience hurt and
sadness as a sheer result of being sensitively present in a world
in which so many people are discontent. Painful feelings often
communicate something about reality when they arise in relation
to those who refuse to grow, or who are quietly suffering –
blind to the possibilities of growth. If we falsely equate personal
development with perpetual happiness, then we will once again
turn against our experience when it contradicts this ideal. Such
an expectation is common, for example, among naive practitioners of meditation, or those who believe that reciting affirm-
ations or practicing positive thinking will lead to an enduring
sense of well-being. Living in a mental realm of positive ideals
can result in a betrayal of our felt experience when such experience seems to contradict a narrow view of how human beings
grow. We then vainly *try* to be happy, instead of effortlessly
allowing happiness to come as a natural result of being caringly
present inside ourselves.

As we open to feeling *more*, we generally begin to feel better.
However, expecting personal growth to mean perpetual happiness would be to sadly miss the point. As we grow, we feel
more, which includes more joy and love, as well as more hurt
and sorrow. However, the good news is that painful feelings are
no longer such a problem when we have learned to be kindly
disposed toward them. In other words, pain is no longer so
painful when we allow it to simply be. We are no longer so

afraid of emotions as we begin to create a context of equanimity in relation to all of our experience.

The unavoidable sorrow that we face in relation to others can, in fact, come to assume a certain quality of richness that borders on joy. Gently opening to the experience of sorrow assumes a vastly different felt quality than the chronic pain associated with resisting our real feelings. Although the English language does not have a word that recognizes the satisfying quality of sad feelings, the Japanese language has a lovely term, 'aware,' which may be translated as 'happy/sad.'[1] Such a sentiment is often depicted in haiku poetry, which beautifully portrays the preciousness of each moment of life, along with the poignant recognition that it too will soon pass, never to return again. In a similar way, the boundary between joy and sorrow becomes less rigidly defined as we learn to be caringly present to all of our felt experience.

HEALING THROUGH REMORSE

While guilt and shame are oppressive experiences generated by self-criticism, the experience of remorse can be a helpful doorway through which to discover more about ourselves. Learning to be caringly present with the felt experience of remorse enables us to recognize when we have hurt a person or neglected to honor our own interests. Hurting another, we may feel sorrowful to realize that we repeatedly neglected to be sensitive to his or her feelings and needs – a pattern that, over time, may have caused this person to leave us. We may also feel remorse for having unwisely neglected our own needs in our misguided attempts to please others or protect them from unavoidable human feelings. Or, we may feel regret for having played it safe, rather than having taken the risk to reach out to a person whom we liked. Or, in a different scenario, we may feel remorseful to have overreacted in a hurtful, angry outburst that was out of proportion to the actual situation. Looking back, we may realize that we were really enraged with some other person, or that we were unrealistically expecting someone to cater to us like a mother or father, instead of simply being a lover or friend.

The experience of remorse can promote growth by pointing toward a state of wholeness or well-being that we could have previously enjoyed had we been more wise, aware, or courageous.

One man, for example, felt remorse for not having been more emotionally available to a woman who loved him; this woman eventually retreated when she realized that her love was unreciprocated. When she eventually married someone else, he felt remorseful to realize he had hesitated because of his attachment to another woman who was not actually available for him, coupled with dissatisfaction regarding her weight. Later, he realized that he actually felt a deep affinity with this woman, and had bypassed an opportunity to develop a loving, intimate relationship with her. Opening to this experience of remorse, rather than blaming her or controlling the feeling through obsessive thoughts, led to a release of bodily held tensions. Following this, he felt a clearer sense of his need for a woman who was really emotionally available to him even though she may not match his romantic images in terms of physical features.

Genuinely felt remorse can touch a deep, tender place inside us. Although sometimes painful to open to at first, it is a rich feeling that can provide a salve that opens the vulnerable, loving place inside us. Touched by remorse, accumulated fears and frustrations can discharge themselves, and we can feel more alive. In addition, we can discover a new alignment with a future direction more in harmony with the deeper longings and aspirations of our being.

Opening to the feeling of remorse can be a refreshing experience that can lead toward the self-forgiveness that is necessary before we can heartily embark upon a new life venture. True remorse may be viewed as a 'corrective' experience. In other words, the very experience of it triggers, in its own time and in its own wise way, some kind of internal realignment that points us toward a more natural, congruent way of being in the world and relating to others. Untinged by unproductive self-blame or self-criticism, remorse can lead to positive life changes not as a result of prodding us or shaming us into submission, but through its own gentle way of showing us a better path – that is, one more in harmony with our organismic need for love, intimacy, and well-being.

Letting go of the guilt and embarrassment generated by the inner critic, and affirming our basic self-worth is a positive, life-enhancing step. A common pitfall, however, is that we may then harden into a stance where we never allow ourselves to feel remorse either. Indignant regarding how we have been manipulated by others or disgusted with ourselves for having been crippled by shame or self-denial for so long, we may react by closing ourselves off to people. While this self-protection may, to some degree, be unavoidable as we first learn to affirm ourselves, we will miss opportunities for contact and deeper intimacy if we solidify into a stance of coldness or arrogance.

For example, if we forget an appointment to meet a friend, we may say to ourselves, 'Why should I feel guilty about that? I didn't mean to inconvenience this person – I just forgot. Everyone forgets sometimes – I'm just human like everyone else. And besides, it's no big deal. Forgetting an appointment doesn't mean I'm bad or unworthy.' There is some useful reasoning here. We certainly do not need to condemn ourselves for missing an appointment. However, the fact remains that we may have hurt this person in some way.

Rather than maintaining a self-righteous or cavalier attitude toward this event, we may experience a greater sense of richness by being sensitive to our friend's feelings. We may then notice that we feel some sadness or remorse for inconveniencing our friend. Sharing this feeling through a statement such as, 'I felt sad that I hung you up,' can be a congruent expression of our remorse. This could lead to a vulnerable and meaningful moment of contact, resulting in a restoration of caring and respect and a renewed sense of closeness.

PART III

Toward the experience of love and intimacy

CHAPTER 8
Trust: a foundation for intimacy

THE COURAGE TO RISK

Allowing ourselves to be vulnerably open to a full range of felt experience requires the courage to take intelligent risks. The word 'courage' derives from the Latin root 'cor', meaning heart. Being courageous means acting with heartfelt integrity even though we may fear unknown consequences; we step forward while acknowledging our fear and allowing ourselves to experience it, rather than attempting to squelch it or pretend it does not exist. Courageously accepting it, we are no longer incapacitated by it.

Whether we are interested in initiating a relationship, confronting issues that are perpetuating dissatisfaction with a current one, or separating from one that is not meeting our needs, being courageous means that we are willing to take the risk to face potentially scary outcomes. We may jeopardize the safe (although stagnant) relationship we have. We may be criticized or ostracized by others for making choices they deem inappropriate. We may feel humiliated or embarrassed. We may find ourselves alone.

Taking risks exposes us to these and other undesirable possibilities. However, as we learn to take care of ourselves by being with a full spectrum of potential feelings that derive from the unpredictability of life, we become more willing to take additional risks toward the actualization of our deepest hopes and longings. It is only by doing so that we may encounter a sensitive response that meets our needs for intimacy and fulfills our yearnings for growth.

TAKING RISKS REQUIRES A LEAP OF FAITH

Facing unknown outcomes requires living with a realistic degree of faith. Having no definite guarantees, we act anyway. We welcome a new adventure. We gently open to something new and mysterious.

Developing a grounded quality of faith in ourselves or in the life process of which we are a part can empower us to grow toward our ever-greater human potential. Although the term 'faith' is usually restricted to religious uses, we find that it contains a crucial psychological aspect that is frequently overlooked. In recognition of its important role in creating meaningful relationships we will now more fully discuss the significance of maintaining an 'intelligent' sense of faith, as opposed to a narrow identification with beliefs.

Although faith is commonly confused with 'beliefs,' it is actually quite the opposite. Beliefs involve a constriction – a narrow attachment to a set of ideas, commonly born out of the mind's desperate attempt to create a semblance of order out of chaos. Unable to tolerate an openness to the larger mystery of life (along with its accompanying anxieties) we may align with beliefs that comfort us with the illusion that we have some kind of sophisticated understanding, scientific proof, secret knowledge, or sacred revelation. Although there may be some elements of truth that lead to the formation of these beliefs, we may lose a basic openness to the mystery of life by becoming proudly attached to our convictions. As a result of our assumed understandings, we experience the comforting illusion that we are in control, rather than the reality of our vulnerability to unpredictable forces in a world beyond our capacity to fully comprehend.

The negative effects of being anchored to our beliefs can be seen most clearly in the realm of organized religion. Although espousing a common message of love, patience, and forgiveness, there is no greater arena for divisiveness, arrogance, and hostility than between opposing religious factions. This is particularly apparent in the Middle East and Ireland, as well as among popular fundamentalist groups that have smug explanations for what, in fact, are the great mysteries of life. Their confidence mostly stems from an unshakable belief in the literal translations of religious texts to which they are dogmatically devoted. The ideas espoused in these books then replace personal experience as the primary source of understanding. As a result, there is an avoidance of one's own experience in the attempt to fit into an approved belief structure. When personal experience does not correspond with these beliefs, there follows a betrayal of the experiencing process itself in favor of a more secure mental/intellectual identity. This leads to a further entrenchment in 'safe' belief structures that are sadly alienated from actual felt experience.

Maintaining control over our lives through fixed beliefs reflects a serious lack of faith in the validity of our own feelings. Separating ourselves from the ongoing process of experiencing has negative implications regarding our ability to feel intimate with others. By abandoning our experience in favor of a mental set of assumptions, we flee from the very place within ourselves where true intimacy is felt. Becoming comfortably wrapped up in beliefs and ignoring our own experience, we bypass an essential doorway through which to feel close to others which, curiously enough, is a central goal of most religions. In short, being identified with beliefs rather than honoring the primacy of our organismic experience, we become impotent to truly love our neighbor (not to mention truly loving ourselves).

Aside from the religious arena, the suffocating effects of beliefs can also be observed in regard to our typical reactions to one another. We tend to quickly form opinions about others, assume we understand their motives, and, when conflicts arise, insist that we are right. This tendency to self-righteously relegate others to a mental slot in our minds is one of the most hurtful and destructive reactions that we impose on each other.

Forming critical beliefs about another's character or shortcomings keeps us a safe distance from the ill-defined pain, hurt, or anxiety we might feel if we maintained an abiding respect and sensitivity for another's humanity. Then, instead of separating ourselves from another and insisting that we are right, sane, or saintly while he or she is wrong, sick, or stubborn, we could take a more humble position of simply sharing our felt experience. This requires considerable courage because it places us in a vulnerable position. Instead of reverting to our self-protecting assumptions, we take a risk to share how we feel; doing so exposes us to being hurt again, but it might also open a channel to increased communication and intimacy.

Beliefs tend to separate us from ourselves and life itself. They also typically lead to divisiveness among individuals, isolation within communities, and conflict between nations. On the other hand, taking the leap of faith to share our real experience with a person is more likely to lead toward a fundamental discovery of our shared human feelings and values, along with a growing trust that we are in safe company.

Living with faith entails suspending beliefs (or at least holding them tentatively), as well as letting go of control over how others may view or respond to us. We then act while acknowledging our legitimate fears about whether we will be respected or accurately perceived by another. We request to spend time with a person, make a risky phone call, express a feeling of resentment, or share a sentiment of appreciation with the faith that by taking a step that feels right to us, we open the possibility for greater love and intimacy. And if we are not well-received, we can rest assured that we acted from our deepest sense of integrity, and, if nothing else, we are at least clearer about where we stand in relation to a particular person. As a result, we can now move ahead in our lives with that new awareness, and allow ourselves to heal by being compassionate toward whatever hurt or sadness is left. And we can feel good about ourselves for having taken a risk for the sake of our growth.

Reaching out to others by taking an intelligent leap of faith is often the first crucial step toward the awakening of a felt trust with another. Whereas an act of faith involves an active dimension of opening toward our own feelings or those of another person, the experience of trust is largely one of settling back into ourselves and allowing a certain kind of connection to develop. This trust develops as we feel safe to be ourselves with another person. We can then feel confident to share an honest emotion, express ourselves spontaneously, or even make an embarrassing mistake.

The experience of trust cannot be created through manipulation or an act of will. Rather, it is something delicate that gradually forms between people. It can certainly be strengthened or weakened by what we do and say (or neglect to do and say), but we cannot directly control it. We can identify and work toward resolving whatever feelings or issues get in the way of a growing sense of trust, but it cannot be forged through a decision that is purely mental.

As we begin to feel the stirrings of trust with another person, we feel safer to take additional risks that further expose our vulnerability. As our risk-taking bears fruit, we feel progressively more confident to further open ourselves and reveal our true feelings, communicate our private thoughts and values, and be ourselves. In short, the more that trust grows, the safer we feel to take further risks in the direction of being fully seen by another, leading to a deepening of intimacy.

'Deciding' to trust a person usually leads to considerable hurt and disappointment if we surrender to intimate contact before this real sense of trust has had time to naturally develop. This premature surrender is an example of blind trust, as opposed to an intelligent, felt trust. Blind trust is oblivious to our experiential sense of the other person, and may overlook reservations or unclear feelings we may be having in relation to him or her. These reservations are frequently bypassed when we feel so deprived of love and intimacy that we quickly grab onto whatever nurturing becomes available. Doing so, however, we remain blind to disconcerting feelings which, if examined, might pose a threat to the relationship. However, these subtle feelings often contain vital messages which, when shared with another, could begin to build a genuine sense of felt trust.

THE INGREDIENTS OF TRUST

Honesty

The capacity and willingness to be honest with others forms a fertile ground from which trust can grow. We trust people who are honest with us. Honest communication is a 'capacity' in the sense that we can only be straightforward with others to the degree that we are able to be honest with ourselves. Being removed from personal feelings, the meaning of these feelings, or what we want from others, we fail to have the clarity of awareness necessary to communicate these in a direct, accurate, and effective manner. Accordingly, honesty is best seen as a relative, rather than absolute, phenomenon. Since self-awareness is relative, our capacity for complete honesty is always a function of our personal development and our degree of self-awareness in any given moment.

The understanding of honesty as a relative phenomenon can help clarify much of the confusion that characterizes this commonly misunderstood term. For instance, the familiar concern that others are being dishonest with us may miss the point. Some communications may be black and white when they involve simple statements of facts or sharing of information; however, in other instances, people may be communicating as honestly as they presently know how. The capacity for total honesty is limited by the unclear feelings, hidden motives, and vague fears that generate much of what we say to one another.

Understanding and accepting our own and other people's limitations may lead to greater feelings of tolerance and empathy. Instead of making unfair accusations (which weaken trust), or misapprehending another's intentions, we may be more inclined to dialogue with the goal of helping one another become clearer about what is true for each of us. Focusing can be an extremely useful tool in this regard, insofar as it helps us become clearer concerning our real feelings so that we may then express these more effectively to others.

Carl Rogers, one of the founding fathers of Humanistic Psychology, uses the term 'congruence' to refer to an accurate matching of our communication with our felt experience in the moment. In other words, our expressions are congruent to the extent that they reflect our real feelings. This is not such an easy undertaking, as Rogers reminds us: 'Being real involves the difficult task of being acquainted with the flow of experiencing going on within oneself, a flow marked especially by complexity and continuous change.'[1] In order to be real with others, we must be aware of what we are feeling from moment to moment. Only through such awareness can we communicate what is really happening inside us.

When other people are incongruent, we tend to feel uncomfortable and untrusting in their presence. For example, while conversing with a man who is telling you about a recent marital separation, you might feel bewildered to notice an occasional smile darting across his face. You imagine that he must be feeling hurt or sad, but all he reveals is a controlled calmness or a pretense of good humor about a painful event.

If, on the other hand, we sense that people are being congruent with us — sharing their feelings and perceptions in an honest, 'sober' way — we tend to notice ourselves beginning to like and trust them; we feel good being with such people. And if this honest, congruent communication is reciprocated, a foundation of trust develops, along with a basis for developing a meaningful relationship.

Being honest with others reflects a faith in their capacity to hear what is true for us, as well as a faith that the relationship can withstand such truth. It also represents a mature understanding that genuine intimacy can only be created in a climate where two individuals are willing to be real with one another. Sensing that others are being misleading, deceitful, or withholding of the full truth, we tend to feel uneasy, suspicious, or resentful. Trust falters and we feel unsafe to be with such people because we are not being responded to in an authentic manner. We are not being treated seriously; our integrity is insulted.

Our experience reveals that most people want to be told the truth, even though it may at times be distasteful or frightening. For example, it is common for people to tell us that they understand how we feel or to nod their heads in apparent agreement when they really do not understand or agree with us at all. We may then be left with an uneasy suspicion regarding their honesty or integrity. A trusting relationship is more likely to develop if others are willing to sensitively tell us that they do not agree with us or do not fully understand what we mean. We feel more trusting recognizing that a relationship is based upon honesty, rather than a 'pseudo-intimacy' in which we pretend to accommodate to one another when, in fact, there are serious misunderstandings, reservations, or disagreements. Taking the risk to share our bewilderment or ask clarifying questions can lead to rich moments of human contact as further dialogue results in being genuinely 'seen' and understood.

Acceptance

In addition to an appreciation of honesty, we tend to be more trusting when we feel accepted. The need to be accepted is largely a matter of wanting to be included and wanting our feelings to be acknowledged and honored. Abraham Maslow refers to this as the basic need to belong – the desire to feel unconditionally accepted without needing to prove ourselves or demonstrate our worth through obedience, cleverness, or accomplishments.

You have probably met people with whom you feel instantly comfortable and at ease. Although, at the time, you may not have fully comprehended why you felt good with such individuals, it is often because of their ability to like and accept you as you are. You feel gratified as you are treated with genuine warmth and kindness.

It is no mystery why this mutual liking does not extend as widely as we might like. Rather than being warm and accepting during social encounters, many of us are busily trying to get people to like us, or maneuvering to display what we think are our strengths, while concealing what we believe to be weaknesses. Becoming preoccupied with a hidden agenda to gain people's acceptance or approval, we often neglect to simply enjoy being with them in a natural, effortless, unpretentious way – a way that would instill a sense of trust.

Having difficulty enjoying relaxed interpersonal contact is accentuated when a weak inner caretaker leads to negative feelings about ourselves. It is difficult to feel at ease with others when we hold the assumption that we are not okay, and that others are somehow more important or powerful. Feeling ashamed or inferior prevents us from enjoying an amiable mutuality that comes only through feeling equal with others in the sense that we are all worthwhile, lovable human beings. The more we come to accept ourselves, the less distracted we are by an insistent need to prove our worth. As a result, our attention can then turn more easily toward being with others in an accepting, caring way. We can then more readily listen to others with a non-judgmental attention that promotes trust.

Feeling uncertain about our own acceptability or worthiness accounts for much of the antagonism and conflict that leads to mistrust. It is when we inwardly view ourselves as inferior or undeserving that we compensate by blaming, criticizing, or verbally attacking others as a way to bolster our sagging self-esteem. We may feel temporarily relieved to imagine that others are as 'screwed up' as we deem ourselves to be. However, trying to feel good by making others feel bad is likely to succeed only in causing hurt or resentment. As a result it is unlikely that they will then feel safe enough to accommodate us with the acceptance we really desire.

Interestingly, we are more sensitive than we often realize. We tend to feel hurt when others judge or disapprove of us, even when such disapproval is not verbally expressed. Being sensitively present to those who hold unspoken negative evaluations of us, we may subtly register their disapproval as a vaguely felt discomfort or an awkward sense of separation.

Whether verbalized or not, critical judgments create an environment hostile to the generation of trust. We tend to become either combative with such people, or to withdraw from them entirely. It is obviously difficult, as well as unwise, to continue to risk being vulnerable with those who continually fail to accept us as we are.

Feeling accepted and cared about, interpersonal trust can grow in the direction of providing a safe context within which disagreements or differences can exist. As this context of mutual acceptance develops, we may feel safe to reveal feelings or thoughts that we might normally hide, such as feelings of hurt or reservations about a relationship.

Comforted by the realization that we can trust another person, we can relax more and more into our real selves. Feeling accepted frees us to fully be ourselves; we no longer have to pursue approval by acting, thinking, or feeling in a prescribed manner. And, interestingly, as we become more congruent, we become easier to like and accept.

Respect

The capacity to accept and care for another person does not mean that we overlook or ignore obvious differences in values, beliefs, or points of view. There may be circumstances under which conflicting perspectives are too great to foster a natural deepening of intimacy between two people. She, for example, may feel strongly about protecting our air and water from industrial pollutants. These environmental values may be in conflict with his perspective that we must protect the free enterprise system from governmental regulations. She may feel that such regulations are necessary because corporations are more interested in profits than controlling the discharge of wastes. He, on the other hand, believes that pollution is the price we pay for progress. In short, there is a clash of values.

It may be difficult to feel intimately connected with someone who sees the world so differently from us. However, a sense of trust can endure by maintaining a respect for the other person's position even if we disagree with it or feel hurt by it. However, if one or both of us feel very strongly about a vital concern, it may be too painful to maintain a deep friendship or move toward a serious commitment due to the other's lack of support for a value we feel so intimately connected with. While mutual trust may be preserved by maintaining broad-minded respect for the other's values, we may also feel drawn to part company.

Holding high respect, even though we oppose another's values or goals, or disagree with a chosen means to reach a similar end, is considerably easier if we perceive that the other has a carefully considered perspective, and is open to re-evaluating his or her position as new information or points of view are offered. If we sense that a person has reflected deeply on his or her own experience and the realities of the external world, we are more likely to retain an abiding respect that keeps trust alive and leaves the door open for further communication.

It is self-defeating, if not humanly impossible, to maintain respect for a value or position that threatens our autonomous right to decide our own destiny. It is painfully contradictory to respect another's point of view if it disrespects the right to our own viewpoint or freedom to make important personal decisions. This contributes to many people's strong distrust of Communism, which is perceived as wanting to impose economic and political values whether or not they are freely chosen. Conversely, many people distrust Capitalism because of its efforts to reap profits while denying workers their right to a proportional share of them. And so we have a highly volatile international situation, created by a sad lack of trust and a failure to honor positions that each side finds very difficult to accept. In another example, lack of respect for human autonomy is one reason why the abortion issue is such an emotional one. Many women experience the anti-choice position as one that would deny them their right to decide their own biological and social future. Viewing these social and political issues from the perspective of a threat to an inalienable right to autonomy, it is no wonder that they raise concerns that generate such deep resentment and mistrust, if not hatred.

Although we may be unaware or unwilling to respect another's political position or personal values, we may at least maintain respect for their basic humanness. This ability to hold another's humanness separate from their beliefs is a difficult discrimination to maintain. However, as we learn the art of being a friendly caretaker for our own feelings, we can develop the capacity to respect the basic integrity of other people, even if we find their beliefs or values offensive.

Initiating or building trust in our relationships can be greatly accelerated by giving up our desire to control another and, instead, making a commitment to uphold each other's basic autonomy. This reciprocal support implies a respect for differences and a mutual trust that we will be accepted and cared about for the feelings and values that derive from our felt experience. We feel safer knowing that another's respect for us does not hinge upon conformity to his or her lifestyle, values, or beliefs, but is based upon a recognition that we are living our own lives with the highest degree of integrity of which we are capable.

Maintaining such respect, even if we do not understand or endorse another's world view, can demonstrate an abiding faith that on some underlying level, a deeper connection unites us in our humanness, even though we may not have a tangible sense of our interconnectedness at the present time. More specifically, we have observed that those who connect with progressively deeper dimensions of felt experience seem to discover an underlying reality that unites all of us in our longing for the ultimate fulfillment of similar needs and aspirations. The majority of our differences then appear to lie in our present choices regarding how to best move toward realizing these shared aspirations, whether individually, or as a community or nation.

Although you may feel pain or sadness to acknowledge your lack of contact or alignment with others, trust can still grow by refraining from the tendency to judge or ridicule others (as well as not taking your non-verbalized judgments seriously). As people feel respected, rather than rejected or controlled, they are granted the freedom to be themselves; trust develops in such an environment.

Maintaining respect for another person's autonomous right to make free choices and hold personal values based upon his or her own felt experience reflects a position of humility. In truth, we do not know what is best for another person. We have enough trouble dealing with our own needs and choices from day to day! Presuming to know another's needs often reflects a basic mistrust in ourselves. Not trusting our own experience, we are inclined not to grant others the right to follow the beat of a different drummer. Such suspicion may be based on the dual fear that if we truly respect people's choices, they may pursue a path that leads them away from us, and that if we trust ourselves, we might discover a new direction that separates us from others. As a result of mistrusting that we each have an inner caretaker that will guide us toward well-being and the fulfillment of our needs, we may feel compelled to impose externally sanctioned values or standards on everyone. However, real trust never gets a chance to develop under such circumstances because, in reality, it can only come into being once we give up the desire to control another's behavior and, instead, honor his or her freedom of choice. Feeling unhampered by manipulation, a person may begin to trust us as a result of trusting that we respect his or her basic integrity.

Respecting others' autonomous individuality reflects the sane and humble view that we are not privileged guardians of the absolute truth, and that others may have pieces of the truth that we have not yet glimpsed. Granting such respect reflects a mature recognition that we may never fully understand the complexity of factors that leads another to feel or think the way he or she does. Realizing that we may never completely comprehend another person, at least not until trust and love have fully blossomed, our most reasonable alternative is to main-

tain an openness to respect our differences, if not learn from
them.

Being Seen

The quickest and perhaps most reliable way to feel trust with
another is to have the experience of being seen and understood
for who we really are. We are 'seen' when our feelings are
understood, or when something that is meaningful to us is
empathically felt by the other person. For example, during a
couples session, Sandy felt upset to hear that Larry viewed her
as his only source of joy in life. Surprised to observe her crying,
Larry could not understand why she was so sad. When she
explained that this led her to feel an overwhelming pressure of
responsibility for his welfare, Larry began to glimpse how heavy
a burden he was placing upon her and that he needed to lessen
his dependency. During this moment of being seen and understood, Sandy felt considerably relieved, and also had more faith
that Larry could become more self-supportive.

Love is at its deepest when it derives from a direct experience
of another in his or her vulnerable humanness. The love that
ensues from touching another's felt experience is a 'knowing'
love insofar as it involves a 'clear seeing' of the other. Seeing a
person's softer, more tender feelings tends to disarm us as we
are reminded of the soft place inside ourselves where we too are
vulnerable. Being in touch with this tender inner place often
awakens a quiet surge of love and warmth toward the other
person.

Feeling a quality of love that derives from being seen is a
most trustworthy kind of love. Sensing that the other person is
in contact with who we really are, we trust that he or she does
not want to harm us, and, in fact, wants to help us heal and
grow. We may then feel safer allowing ourselves to become
more intimate with such a person.

To truly know and love another in this special way is not a
routine occurrence because it requires the kind of wisdom that
knows how to be deeply empathic. To be internally touched by
another's feelings and personal meanings implies an ability to
temporarily put aside our own needs, quiet the inner chatter

that tends to preoccupy our minds, and totally 'be there' for the other – getting close enough to be, in effect, inside his or her experience. This ability to closely resonate with another's experience develops as we learn to caringly tend to our own feelings and felt meanings. As we learn to 'be there' for ourselves – open and friendly toward our own depths – we likewise become more emotionally available to 'be there' for others.

As our feelings are seen, appreciated, and understood, and as the deeper essence of our being is at least partially or momentarily apprehended, we tend to experience a rapid strengthening of the fabric of trust uniting us with another. The awakening of this trust reflects a profound organismic contact stemming from the very core of our respective beings. Such trust, resulting from the knowledge that we have been clearly seen, provides a foundation from which we feel progressively safer to surrender to ever-deeper levels of love and intimacy.

TRUSTING OUR INTERCONNECTEDNESS

As we nourish and support conditions that lead to an awakening of trust, then even if a relationship falters, it is likely that we will eventually attract others whose needs, values, and perspectives more closely match our own. On the basis of years of psychotherapeutic research, Carl Rogers alludes to this eventuality in an insightful passage from *Person to Person* (1967):

> In persons who are moving toward greater openness to their experiencing, there is an organismic commonality of value directions. These common value directions are of such kinds as to enhance the development of the individual himself, of others in his community, and to make for the survival and evolution of his species.[2]

These value directions, as discussed by Rogers, include being increasingly honest, open, self-affirming, and self-directed. In addition, as we grow, we experience greater acceptance of our own feelings, needs, and reactions, as well as those of others. We would extend this description to include values such as an affirmation of our playful 'inner child,' and a tendency to find satisfaction through experiencing power *with* people rather than *over* them. In addition moving toward closer contact with organismic experience seems to lead to a clearer recognition of the value of finding peace within ourselves and in relation to others, along with a growing appreciation for the beauty and sanctity of nature.

These value directions may be considered 'organismic' ones in the sense that they are likely to be discovered or chosen by all individuals in whatever culture, so long as such individuals feel safe to open to ever deeper levels of felt experience. One of the most important of these value directions that emerges as we befriend our felt experience is a growing interest in establishing a deep, meaningful intimate relationship. The recognition that contacting felt experience leads to the common discovery of the human need for love and intimacy, and beyond that a preference for openness and sensitivity in all our relationships, has some noteworthy implications.

Since human beings seem to ultimately want to actualize a common human potential (even though we may not be so aware of this at the present time), then what may account for many of our current differences is our unique approach toward a mutually desired direction. The realization that our differences or conflicts are largely due to various pathways toward a similar destination is a crucial one because it has the potential to lead to a greater felt unity with our fellow human beings.

As we begin to gain even vague glimpses of an underlying sense of connectedness, we may become more confident to take additional risks in making contact with others. Through a growing awareness that others basically want the same thing that we do, we will feel more empowered to be ourselves, reach out, and accept the risk of rejection. Developing a clearer sense of contact with others through the medium of our shared felt experience, we are likely to have greater respect for personality differences and dissimilar world views. Such differences pale in the light of an underlying felt contact or an intuition regarding the possibilities of genuine contact with others. If each of us is committed to grow toward the depths of our own experience, then these differences tend to become less divisive as we each begin to embody lessons learned from the wisdom contained in our felt experience.

Even if we do not fully connect with someone we are initially attracted to, mutual trust can nevertheless endure through embodying trust-promoting values. We may then part amicably or perhaps continue an acquaintanceship or friendship even if our current differences are discovered to be too great to accommodate a growing intimacy.

Taking a step back from one another in a sensitive manner is not the typical manner of separating in circumstances where one or both individuals have developed a strong attachment to a desired relationship. The common scenario, all too familiar to most of us, is to cut off our vulnerability, withdraw into ourselves, lose trust in the other person, and develop a self-protecting position of blame where we see ourselves 'in the right' and the other person as wrong, untrustworthy, or uncaring.

As we become 'well-practiced' in the art of being friendly toward our own feelings and sensitive in our communications, we develop the capacity to respond to one another in a kinder way if differences become insurmountable, or if incompatibilities become painfully obvious. The possibility then opens for a more sensitive parting of the ways, along with a faith that we *could* meet more fully at a later time (provided we are both committed to being open to our felt experience), since after all, we are similarly growing toward deeper dimensions of what it means to be human.

Whether we completely separate or maintain minimal contact, a time may later arrive when, due to personal growth on the part of one or both of us, we may meet more directly and easily, free of the conflicts that once seemed insurmountable. However, whether or not this future connection occurs, we have parted on good terms, with full respect and caring for one another's ultimate well-being. Even if we never meet again, we can feel a special kind of satisfaction knowing that we have embodied a high degree of integrity throughout the course of a relationship, however brief or lengthy it might have been – the air has been cleared, we learned something of value, and we can feel free to move ahead in our lives. If we encounter the person again, we can, perhaps, discuss old times, enjoy one another's company, and notice our growth from times past. But whether we actually meet or not, we have allowed ourselves to remain inwardly open to one another.

The openness of being that results from our effort to embody

trust-promoting values tends to ultimately reward us wit
quality of love and intimacy we need. As we continue to
toward the realization of our full human potential, we ter
more readily notice those who are moving in a similar direction.
Also, we tend to be more easily recognized by those who glimpse
something vital in us that resonates with their own growth
direction. In short, if we do not continue in a relationship we
are initially drawn to, we are more likely to develop a fulfilling
relationship with someone who is more compatible with us.

SOME 'SPIRITUAL' IMPLICATIONS OF DEVELOPING FAITH AND TRUST

The relationship between individual and interpersonal union has
been explored by Teilhard de Chardin, a paleontologist and
Catholic priest who wrote in the early and mid–1900s. Similar
to Rogers, Teilhard de Chardin (1959) takes a developmental
perspective, and lays an elaborate scientific foundation to help
substantiate his views. To express it briefly, he sees human
consciousness gradually growing in complexity and sensitivity
to a point where we will ultimately recognize our essential unity
of being in what he calls the Omega Point. From his perspective,
recognizing our commonality of purpose and ultimate destination is not merely an intriguing metaphysical possibility, but
a dire necessity for the survival of our species. 'Unite or perish,'
he warns us, recognizing that differences between individuals
and nations have brought us to the brink of a hostile confron-
tation in the nuclear age.

While he does not avail himself of psychological language to
explain his vision, he opens the door to a rich interface between
psychology and religion. Although this study is barely in its
infancy, we are observing that contact with organismic experience, coupled with a discovery of what it takes to form genuinely
deep, loving relationships naturally leads in a direction that has
been called 'spiritual' (whether or not we would choose that
term ourselves).

Not all theologians, of course, support or, more to the point,
even understand Teilhard de Chardin's evolutionary perspective.
Most Christian churches are sadly lacking in the most rudimen-

tary principles of psychological growth and awareness that are necessary for helping people grow toward the felt experience that he conceptualizes so brilliantly. Hidden to the awareness of even the most devout of the clergy, as well as the general population, lie the most profound psychological truths, shrouded in theological concepts that have lost most of their experiential meaning. Rediscovering this meaning can reveal an exciting new dimension to the path of relationships.

For example, the Christian concept of faith, as explained earlier, has largely degenerated into mere belief – a realm of shadows rather than substance. Understood in an experiential framework, faith can mean taking risks to be honest with ourselves and open to life, which implies a willingness to become aware of our actual organismic experience, regardless of whether it is pleasant or anxiety-provoking. Through a wise faith we can also learn to become progressively more open and vulnerable with one another, which can lead to unexpected avenues of growth and fulfillment.

Living with faith is not just a noble spiritual idea – it is the best practical way to discover the trust and intimacy we need. Just as sexual pleasure is heightened as we give up control and surrender to a natural bodily function, so can having the faith to surrender to our honest, more vulnerable feelings lead to the joy of experiencing loving contact with others.

Being supported by a safety net of trust that can accommodate the tender growth of love is not something we can consciously manipulate or actively control. We can, however, make certain efforts that may lead to the awakening of trust and love. This is where faith enters. It is the kind of faith that leads to an affirmation of our actual felt experience, as well as the willingness to risk reaching out from that experience in a congruent manner, which opens the possibility that trust will grow.

'Grace' is another theological term that has important meaning when applied to the experiential realm of relationships. 'Grace' has been defined as something precious that comes to us which we have absolutely no control over. Similarly, we cannot accurately predict or guarantee whether we will be loved by others; they are free to love us or not. Love and intimacy can be viewed as coming through grace – we have no ultimate control over whether we will feel this with any particular individual. However, we can do more than the traditional Christian perspective recognizes. Through understanding some of the conditions under which trust grows and intimacy flourishes, we can move courageously ahead to create such circumstances.

TRUSTING OTHERS, LIFE, AND OURSELVES

An additional dimension of relationships unfolds as we realize that trusting others goes hand in hand with trusting life itself. We cannot, in fact, grow toward deeply trusting others unless we also begin to trust the larger life context in which our relationships exist. Life has curious ways of bringing us potential lessons through the significant relationships we form with people, however short-lived they may be.

Distrusting the experiences life brings us, we are inclined to be cynical and 'on guard' as we meet people or face life events. Facing unpleasant experiences, we may blame others or conclude that life is unfair or hostile. Learning to trust the life process can inspire us to affirm the experiences that come to us as a result of being alive, learn what they have to offer, and move confidently ahead in our lives, somewhat wiser than before. The life process then becomes, in a sense, our teacher.

Our capacity to trust others is also enhanced to the degree that we learn to trust ourselves. Such trust, in its deepest sense, involves trusting that we can deal with the feelings that arise in us as we encounter life experiences. Knowing that we are willing to face and accept such feelings, whether pleasant or unpleasant, empowers us to confidently relate to people. This is not to say that we foolishly trust people who repeatedly fail to return our trust, but that we are better able to at least give people a fair chance if we trust that we can be a caretaker for our hurt or sorrow if our overtures are unreciprocated. Trusting ourselves in this way enables us to maintain an emotional availability to others that could lead to enjoyable contact or an important learning experience.

As we discover that many life situations we encounter are 'grist for the mill' of our personal growth, we tend to become more trusting of life, less fearful and defensive, and more open to our experience. Then, whether we are dealing with an interpersonal relationship or some other important issue such as work or the search for meaning in our lives, we can move forward with greater trust and courage.

Growing in faith and trust can expand within three crucial dimensions of experience: our relationship with other people, with the larger life process, and with ourselves. As we feel a greater confidence and trust in any one of these areas, we tend to develop and strengthen essential inner qualities that help us feel more at home in the other two dimensions as well. For example, if we are feeling weary or wounded in relation to others, we can tap the strength of our trustworthy inner care-taker. Trusting that we have the capacity to heal within ourselves can generate a quiet strength to once again take risks in relation to trusting others. As we enjoy the rewards of satisfying interpersonal contact and as we learn helpful lessons that enable us to move forward in our lives, we learn to trust the larger life process to guide us toward further experiences that can continue to help us grow. In addition, the more we trust life, the more we come to trust the interpersonal needs that life brings up in us – which invites us to find ways to create the trusting contact that would fulfill these needs and enable us to grow. And the more fulfilled and supported we feel as the result of a growing trust with others, the easier it is to love ourselves and trust that we really *can* meet our growth needs.

Trusting life also frees us from the unhealthy tendency to cling to one partner as our only source of fulfillment. Intimate relationships eventually lose their vitality when we contract into an exclusive dependence upon one other person. If, in the course of time, we neglect to extend the energies of love and our newly found sense of trust toward others and toward life in general, including our work and other relationships, we can smother trust and intimacy by continuing to look to the relationship for some kind of ultimate gratification or 'salvation.' Then, instead of further actualizing ourselves by extending our trust and love, we may use the relationship to avoid the pain or hurt that might result from risking this further opening.

Teilhard de Chardin's call to 'unite or perish' may be more clearly understood in the light of our tendencies to contract into a narrow relationship with our spouse, friend, hoped-for mate, or biological family, as opposed to heeding life's call to widen our attention to include the greater human community. This is not to suggest that we can form intimate relationships with everyone in the world. But it does mean that our need to grow as individuals and as a species may be facilitated by moving toward an emotional attitude that includes rather than excludes others. As a result, we may open to an increasing degree of love and intimacy with more than our partner or our immediate family, as long as the form of this contact supports our primary commitments.

The tendency to withdraw into ourselves or protect narrow personal interests that provide a modicum of security or comfort is, for Teilhard de Chardin, the real meaning of the Christian term, 'sin.' As he expresses it, sin is the 'refusal to love;' this separates us from one another, from ourselves, and from the larger mystery called 'God.' Expanding this further into experiential terms, we might say that what Christians are trying to express by the term 'sin' is actually an unwillingness to be vulnerably present with our genuinely felt experience, coupled with a refusal to risk honestly sharing that experience in an open exchange. Understanding this can provide the sorely needed experiential underpinnings to a complicated theology that continues to dominate the lives of most people in the Western world. [3]

Uniting with others can become a distinctly felt reality, instead of merely an intriguing possibility, as we become real and vulnerable with each other. And, as suggested earlier, we can be open to others only to the degree that we are in contact with our own felt experience – that is, to the degree that we trust ourselves to be in touch with ourselves. Therefore, overcoming our 'sins', or, as we prefer to say, learning to make genuine contact with others, requires an intention to become aware of our actual felt experience, followed by a befriending of that experience and an openness to communicating with others. Any religion that promotes doctrines or beliefs that are not integrated with this experiential dimension may be actively hurting people by encouraging a life-negating split between mental ideas and bodily-felt experience.[4]

The 'openness' to make contact with others by sharing our felt experience does not necessarily mean that we *always* express how we feel, which can become a compulsion, insensitive to how others may receive our sharing. But it does mean that we are not withdrawing or holding back in a stance of self-protection; we are open to expressing ourselves as we experience the 'rightness' of it in any given situation. The most skillful action is not always easy to determine; in fact, it is extremely difficult to discern what will best serve the well-being of both ourselves and others. That is why 'sin' is such an unskillful word, unless we view it simply as 'missing the mark' (from its original Greek root). Removing the punitive quality of the word 'sin' can help us better understand the reality to which it points – the fact that we can always come closer and closer to the mark. That is, we can usually be somewhat more in touch with ourselves and with the larger life process, and more empathically present to others. In fact, our capacity to experience love, compassion, and intimate contact with others may be boundless.

Teilhard de Chardin's call to 'unite' with others cannot occur through an heroic act of will. But as we create conditions under which we feel safer with one another, a felt sense of trust and love naturally unfolds. Growth toward an embodied spirituality may then develop as a natural outgrowth of implementing the intimacy-building approaches that we have been discussing. These include contacting our felt experience, recognizing our need for love and intimacy, taking a leap of faith into our child-like vulnerability, creating a safe environment for mutual openness, making friends with our aloneness, being willing to tolerate both pleasant and unpleasant feelings within ourselves, and learning to communicate in a sensitive, skillful, non-judgmental way. Embodying these aspects of experience eases us in a direction where we may discover a crucial interface between sound emotional development and mature spiritual growth. In fact, whether or not we are inclined to use the overworked term 'spiritual,' learning to live in this manner naturally moves us toward embodying values and experience that lie at the very heart of all the major spiritual traditions.

RELEARNING TRUST

Our early experiences in relation to our parents, significant adults, and peers play critical roles in determining the degree to which we are presently able to take risks with others. If we were fortunate enough to be raised in a trust-promoting environment – recipients of generous portions of honesty, acceptance, and respect – then taking leaps of faith in regard to being open to others tends to be less scary and a more natural part of life. If our previous risk-taking as vulnerable children was rewarded with plentiful acceptance and love, we tend to be more confident about reaching out and more trusting in the life process. Most of us, unfortunately, did not grow up in such an open and nurturing environment.

Lacking a necessary degree of faith in life and confidence in relation to opening to others, our risk-taking assumes a more serious, guarded tone. The risks are greater and the stakes higher because we were not taught how to take refuge within ourselves and be our own best friend. Also, having little trust in life, we tend to feel easily betrayed when we get hurt in a relationship. We are then prone to blame others, rail against life, or sink into apathy and depression if our vulnerable overtures are met with rejection. Such an outcome may further solidify a self-protecting assumption that life is 'just very difficult' and people are not to be trusted.

Assessing the degree to which we learned genuine trust in our families is a difficult task. Human beings are endowed by nature with marvelous psychological mechanisms to survive the pain, isolation, or emotional desolation of childhood. We learn to endure an environment hostile to the creation of trust. This being the case, we may become conveniently numb to the lack of trust, love, and intimacy in our lives, and may rely upon various addictions or substitute gratifications in order to deal with this sad fact.

RELEARNING TRUST THROUGH A THERAPEUTIC RELATIONSHIP

The therapeutic relationship can be an effective way to relearn trust. Through the safety provided by this relationship, we may explore barriers to trust and learn to risk being vulnerable. As we are gently guided toward our felt experience, the source of inner and outer conflicts may slowly unravel and we may gradually learn to love and befriend ourselves.

The therapeutic relationship provides a special context in which feelings and meaningful issues tend to arise within us and also in relation to the therapist. Healing and growth can accelerate as we build an ever-deepening foundation of trust with both the therapist and ourselves. As this trust strengthens, it is easier to risk exploring and sharing our real feelings. And as our vulnerable sharing is sensitively received, we grow to trust even more.

Growth involves risks, of course, even in a therapeutic setting, and emotional healing requires a span of time that cannot be reliably predicted. But the advantage of placing faith in the therapeutic relationship is that the therapist (at least one who is both competent and empathic) is a person who is skilled in helping individuals explore obstacles to trusting themselves and others. In addition, skilled therapists are individuals who, in the best of cases, are not only professionally competent but are also committed to their own personal growth, which includes the embodiment of trust-building values. We say 'in the best of cases' because many traditionally trained therapists are not necessarily committed to integrating such values into their personal lives. Clients can often sense this split between a therapist's professional stance and commitment to personal growth. The perception that the therapist is more involved in 'wearing' a particular therapeutic model than embodying a vulnerable human presence rightly interferes with trusting the therapist at a depth that is necessary for substantial therapeutic progress.

Although the trend began to change in the mid–1960s, many therapists, psychologists, and especially psychiatrists continue to adhere to the limiting medical model perspective. Troubled individuals are often viewed as having 'mental disorders' or 'illness.' These terms represent a mental counterpart to physical disease, the traditional domain of Western medicine. Unfortunately, however, to apply principles of conventional medicine to the mental/emotional realm of our being is to overlook the vastness of what it means to be human. Then, instead of addressing and exploring the more complex emotional and spiritual issues that are often at the core of our discontents, health professionals resort to 'treatment strategies' and an array of psychotherapeutic techniques and chemical interventions. These medical approaches are applied to what is often really a problem in living – ones that we are all struggling with to varying degrees.

In our opinion, psychotherapeutic approaches based upon the traditional medical model frequently perpetuate the underlying problem through their fundamental stance of professional distancing, pathologizing the 'patient' and utilizing strategies and techniques as substitutes for embodying a vulnerable, human presence. This approach sets up a questionable power dynamic between the 'therapist' and the one called 'patient' that can complicate the individual's difficulties by reinforcing the notion that there is something terribly 'wrong' with him or her.[5] In contrast, a more 'therapeutic' and helpful perspective may be one in which both the therapist and the individual are viewed as human beings who have various strengths and limitations. Such an attitude could help diffuse a deep-seated belief that is contributing to the person's original difficulties, namely, that he or she is somehow sick or inferior. Interacting with an individual in a genuinely human, congruent manner can become a primary source of growth by creating a relationship in which the therapist models a stance of vulnerability and healthy human interaction.

As a result of these various considerations, it is suggested that anyone who seeks a counselor or therapist be extremely selective in their choice. We advise interviewing several therapists before making a commitment to such an intimate process (and a commitment is very helpful, once some degree of trust has been established with the therapist). After one or more sessions with a particular therapist, we suggest that you consider questions such as: 'Do I feel good with this person? Do I sense that I can trust him or her? Does he or she seem to respect and encourage the growth of my autonomy? Are my choices respected? Are interpretations of my behavior or feelings offered tentatively or are they insisted upon? Does the therapist help me explore my feelings, or is he or she quick to tell me what they mean?'

If you feel good about the person, you may benefit by remaining in the therapeutic process for some appropriate length of time, rather than leaving at the first signs of difficulty. If you begin to experience reservations or mistrust in the therapist, we suggest that you discuss your feelings openly with him or her.

In order to make it easier to find a counselor or therapist whose orientation is consistent with the approach outlined in this book, we have included a guide to resources in the appendix. This will serve as a referral source to qualified practitioners in local areas where we can suggest either a workshop or private sessions.

HEALING THROUGH CLOSE RELATIONSHIPS

Apart from a therapeutic relationship, healing and growth can occur through taking informed risks in our closer friendships or intimate relationships. As we allow others to see our real selves, we may discover a growing trust through feeling accepted and appreciated for who we are. As a result, we may relax more and more as we feel safer to allow deeper fears, hurts, or other vulnerable feelings to spontaneously emerge. We may also feel relieved to share opinions and express values that we may have kept hidden due to a fear of rejection or humiliation if we dared divulge them.

We grow as we feel free to fully be ourselves. By accepting and loving others as they presently are, instead of holding back until they meet our idealized images or romantic expectations, they may feel a sense of safety that finally enables them to release the pain of past hurts. These accumulated bodily held hurts and frustrations, which often originate from previous rejection or unreciprocated love, have an opportunity to heal within the new context of a relationship characterized by a growing sense of trust. Such a relationship may then become a 'therapeutic' one in that we are resolving conflicts and growing toward a healthier, happier dimension of being.

CHAPTER 9
Self-revealing communication: a vital bridge between two worlds

The gradual awakening of trust between two individuals is a delicate and precarious process – even a seemingly stable relationship can be jeopardized by unanticipated forces. We have already discussed how mistrust can develop from an absence or lapse of trust-building factors. Trust can also be neutralized or eroded by sad failures of communication that can have unfortunate, and even tragic consequences. We will now explore how skillful communication can help generate the vital sense of safety, mutual understanding, and respect that is so necessary for enhancing trust and intimacy.

Effective communication begins with a willingness to be honest with ourselves. We cannot express our real feelings or share what is meaningful for us unless we are prepared to take a sober look inside ourselves and ascertain what is true for us. Communication becomes more effective as we develop the courage to acknowledge our real feelings and reactions, including potentially scary or painful shades of our felt experience. The Focusing process, through its ability to encourage underlying layers of experience to reveal themselves, can be a helpful tool for facilitating the elusive self-awareness that is so essential for human communication.

Becoming aware of our felt experience leads to the next step of conveying that experience to another. This may be done through verbal expression that reflects inner experience as accurately as possible. As Focusing becomes a more natural part of our lives, so does expressing the experiences we contact while Focusing. As we learn to attend to felt experience moment by moment, it becomes easier to articulate that experience in ways that others are more likely to receive and understand. Communicating feelings is often difficult at first as we experiment with finding words that most accurately express the more poignant aspects of our experience. Through lifelong practice, we can learn to communicate with ever-increasing clarity and effectiveness.

In the meantime, whether we are aware of it or not, revealing messages are conveyed through various nonverbal modes of communicating. Numerous studies have revealed that much communication is nonverbal in nature. Through our facial expression, tone of voice, gestures, body language, and quality of eye contact, we instantly convey a world of feelings and meanings. Though we are often oblivious to these expressions, such nonverbal cues are sometimes more honest and revealing than the verbal comments we make. While words may deceive, our bodies have an uncanny way of expressing the truth, whether we are aware of this or not.

Even if others are not especially perceptive or intuitive, they register our presence at some level of awareness. For example, we may ask the perfunctory question, 'How are you?' when, in reality, we are not really interested in knowing. Sensing that our mechanical question is not genuinely felt, others may automatically respond in a similarly superficial, habitual manner by saying, 'Fine. How are you?' Through nonverbal cues, people can often sense whether we are just being polite or if our social graciousness is sincere and genuinely felt.

Becoming more attuned to nonverbal expressions and the meanings and feelings they convey, you can enter a rich new world of interpersonal contact. As you become more aware of how your body expresses feelings, you can allow eye contact, tone of voice, and gestures to support your words, resulting in communications that are more clear, poignant, and effective. Taking advantage of a full repertoire of available communication modes increases the likelihood of being seen, understood, and positively responded to.

The use of language is the primary vehicle through which we share our inner world of feelings, meanings, values, and thoughts with others. It is a sad fact that many relationships suffer or deteriorate not primarily as a result of major substantive differences, but because of unskillful communication. Such ineffectual communication can then further complicate whatever emotional difficulties or interpersonal conflicts that may be jeopardizing the relationship.

Learning to speak in ways that effectively express feelings and meanings, without attacking others or undermining their autonomy, requires attention to important details of language and how to best convey our felt experience to others. Unfortunately, most parents did not teach this skill to their children – they never learned it themselves. Educators, being the product of a culture unschooled in the realm of feelings, are also poorly prepared to teach this important skill. As a result, public education has developed a momentum that blithely continues to promote academic skills leading to successful careers and material progress. Tragically, however, virtually nothing has been done to educate us regarding the critical human realities of relationships, marriage, and family life. During the past few decades, psychologists and educators have been carefully exploring the key elements involved in effective communication. We now understand many of the principles that lead to skillful communication, as well as factors that contribute to misunderstanding and mistrust. Implications for non-violent conflict resolution, the growth of loving, intimate relationships and, on a larger scale, the development of a global psychology of peace, are just beginning to be understood.

STRUCTURING OUR LANGUAGE TO INVITE CONTACT

The complex art of verbal communication is a learned skill that can enhance intimacy and mutual understanding when the structure of our language conveys the trust-promoting attitudes of honesty, acceptance, caring, and respect. The ability to state our experience in a simple, direct, noncoercive manner can serve the dual purpose of communicating what is happening in our inner world while honoring other people's right to respond to us in a manner that preserves the integrity of their own felt experience. Integrating this respectful attitude into the very structure of our language can do much to promote trust and create genuine contact between two autonomous individuals.

Thomas Gordon, in a landmark book entitled *Parent Effectiveness Training*, describes how communication is more effective when we express ourselves using, 'I statements' as opposed to 'you statements.' 'I statements,' or what we will call 'self-revealing communications,' are those that disclose our experience without attacking others, invalidating their feelings, or criticizing them for not meeting our needs or conforming to our point of view. Self-revealing communications invite others into our tender world of feelings and meanings. They reflect a willingness to risk being vulnerable, rather than resort to strategies of control or manipulation in order to get what we want.

For example, we might say, 'I'm feeling frustrated about our conversation because I imagine that I'm not being understood.' This way of expression effectively says how we feel, ('frustrated') and gives the additional input of sharing what this feeling means to us ('being misunderstood').

Instead of this self-disclosing communication, we could resort to a variety of what Gordon calls 'you statements,' or what we prefer to call 'intrusive communications.' For example, instead of cleanly communicating that we feel frustrated or sad, we could blame the other person for not understanding us by saying something such as, 'We're not resolving our conflict because you don't listen to my side of the story!' We could also criticize the other by a hostile statement such as, 'You never want to listen to me!' Or, we may wage a personal attack by responding, 'You're really selfish, childish, and stupid!'

The above reactions are impulsive ways of acting out our feelings, as opposed to simply sharing them. This can quickly lead to a downward spiral in the communication process. Mistrust grows and communication falters (if it ever existed in the first place), because people then feel judged rather than respected, criticized instead of accepted, intruded upon rather than invited to openly explore disagreements. Feeling less safe to be open and vulnerable, individuals will tend to react by either increasing their verbal attacks, which can further escalate a counter-productive power struggle, or withdrawing entirely in order to protect themselves from further hurt.

Self-revealing communications reflect a wise willingness to take responsibility for how we feel, rather than transfer blame or make judgmental decrees that infringe upon people's basic humanness. For instance, we may say, 'I feel hurt when you joke about my weight. That's a sensitive area because people have kidded me about it all of my life.' This statement is a simple, open description of how we feel. It also offers information to the other person that may assist him or her in understanding how past experiences have contributed to our present feeling. It does not counter-attack by saying, 'Well, you're pretty flabby, too!' It does not criticize by exclaiming, 'You're always nagging me about my weight.' It does not place demands or pose threats as by stating, 'If you don't stop, you'll be sorry!' All of these intrusive statements are manipulations in that they are intended to coerce the other to change his or her behavior, rather than to simply express our feelings. Such assertions represent a lack of trust in the other person's propensity to respond favorably to us if we reveal our more tender, vulnerable feelings. And, practically speaking, these intrusive statements rarely, if ever, produce lasting changes. Although one or the other may temporarily give in, resentments will continue to mount. As the basic humanness of the organism is wounded by this judgmental, coercive process, a cycle of damaging communications is generated. Allowing this to continue, a relationship can degenerate to the point where all openness and warmth are crushed. The two vulnerable and hurting human beings then take care of themselves the best way they know how – by retreating behind walls of self-protection and defense. However, the periodic eruption of vindictive, embittered fights will reveal the layer upon layer of unresolved resentment, hurt, and mistrust.

For example, one therapy client was convinced that her husband was hopelessly insensitive and that all their marital problems resulted from his selfishness. After a painful separation, followed by considerable reflection, she began to own her side of the problem. Never having experienced a father who was emotionally available, she had been wanting her husband to be the 'good parent' she never had – one who was continuously and selflessly attentive to her needs. Of course, he could never fulfill such fantasies, and eventually became involved with another woman as an escape from the confusion and conflict of his marriage. Unfortunately, their respective differences were never openly discussed. Instead, she self-righteously blamed him inwardly. But rather than communicate her anger directly, she would express it in subtle, hurtful ways that resulted in his feeling disrespected and unloved. He then felt even less inclined to respond to her feelings in a caring way.

Learning to communicate in a more reflective, self-revealing manner can halt a painful escalation of interpersonal tension by removing the fuel that has been intensifying the conflict. Hostilities may then cease long enough for us to explore what is really going on – that is, the unacknowledged feelings, meanings, and unmet needs that are at the source of the difficulties. As these are openly shared, some trust may re-emerge.

Whether we long to heal the wounds with a friend or partner, improve a satisfying relationship, or initiate a new one, self-revealing communications can be instrumental in eliciting responses from others that lead to greater love and intimacy in our lives. Such expressions shine a gentle light on our inner world, offering a glimpse of what we really feel and how we see things. This more self-searching and self-disclosing approach to interpersonal relating holds the prospect that another will treat us with loving care and human sensitivity as we become willing to be transparent. Lowering our defensive shield, we open ourselves to the possibility of being seen and warmly embraced, which is our quiet hope, although we risk being hurt, which is an ever-present possibility.

Focusing attention on the dimension of disclosing our feelings, instead of on the nearly impossible task of trying to change others' behavior, can drastically shift the typical interactional scenario. By simply sharing how we feel in response to people's words or actions, we reveal our hurt, fear, anger, or other vulnerable feelings that are evoked by their words or deeds. Communicating in this way becomes an invitation for others to sensitively respond to our feelings and concerns, and, perhaps, to voluntarily modify their behavior.

A basic assumption behind self-revealing expressiveness is that if people see who we really are, how we really feel, and what we really need, they will tend to respond to us in an accommodating manner; at ground level, people do care about one another, and wish to be helpful if they can. In fact, some studies suggest that empathy is an innate human response.[1]

In order for others to care about us they need to know what we are feeling. And, rather than assume that they already understand or 'should' know how we feel, it is our responsibility to tell them. Self-revealing statements can be an empowering, effective way to communicate feelings and needs. An honest self-disclosing expression of our real feelings can make the crucial difference that leads to greater trust. Being non-manipulative, such expressions encourage others to concretely express their caring for us by allowing themselves to be touched by our feelings, and, as a result, respond to us in a more loving, cooperative way.

By communicating in a more vulnerable, self-revealing manner, we give people a chance to change while respecting their autonomous right to choose whether or not they want to change or give us what we are asking for. If they minimize our concerns, resist communicating about them, or refuse to be touched by our experience, then, of course, we may not feel very safe to continue exposing our vulnerable feelings. Our sense of trust will most likely diminish because we are not receiving caring in the way we need it. A vital, growing relationship requires two individuals who are willing and able to be touched by one another's feelings and be responsive to each other's felt concerns.

The communication of feelings is best done when others have the time and interest to hear what we have to say, rather than trying to make contact during a football game or after a tiring day at work. Eliminating or minimizing the distracting influences of the television, telephone, children, or pets enables us to attend more carefully to our subtle feelings and understand each other's concerns. It is often helpful to set aside time on a regular basis, such as one evening each week, in order to discuss ongoing issues or share recent upsets so that they may be resolved before they grow into more serious conflicts.

Creating undistracted time to open to each other's feelings, can create a refreshingly safe environment in which to become better acquainted with one another, and, as trust builds, to enjoy the flourishing of love and intimacy.

THE POWER OF VULNERABILITY

Although using self-revealing statements to sensitively share our feelings and needs may appear to reduce us to a weaker position in terms of getting what we want from a relationship, in reality, the opposite is true. On the surface, it may seem that we rise to a stronger position by fighting for the changes we would like to see in the other person. We often fool ourselves by thinking that if only we could assert ourselves a little more convincingly or forcefully, then the other person would finally change.

Those who have discovered the hidden power of vulnerability realize that being vulnerable does not mean being weak. In fact, a special kind of inner strength is required to 'hold our own' as we experience and assert our genuine feelings, as opposed to aggressively reacting with blame, attacks, moralizing, or other forms of manipulation that create an adversarial position. Even the intense emotion of anger can be expressed 'cleanly' without being contaminated by blame, criticism, or self-righteousness.

As we learn to caringly accommodate our softer feelings, we can breathe more deeply and take greater risks in relation to others. Feeling strong and confident within ourselves, our communications can embody an integrity that respects another's freedom of response while affirming our right to our feelings and to make crucial life decisions based upon our growth needs.

Responding from a confident center within our vulnerable inner world reflects a special kind of inner strength. Reacting in a demanding or hostile way usually masks a personal sore spot or long-term unexpressed and unsatisfied need. What is sometimes considered to be a 'strong' or courageous position often camouflages a host of unacknowledged fears or unexplored areas within ourselves that we have yet to understand, accept, or befriend.

For example, Rose, who wanted the best for her son, Ira, pressured him to enter medical school, which he reluctantly agreed to do. Finding the stresses of school overwhelming, he wanted to drop out, a decision his mother found difficult to accept. Needing her love and respect (and having an undeveloped inner caretaker), he agreed to push ahead in school. Shortly thereafter, Ira died of cancer. Only then was Rose able to acknowledge her fear of being embarrassed or ashamed if her son did not enter a prestigious profession.

What seemed a strong position by Rose was actually a reaction to her unexplored fears of being an inadequate parent. Unskilled at contacting and communicating her more vulnerable feelings, and unwilling to trust Ira to make decisions consistent with his own best interests, she remained invested in her own decision regarding what he should do. This led to pressuring him in ways that she later regretted.

Trying to achieve resolution on the dimension of feelings, rather than being preoccupied with what we think is the 'right' thing for someone to do (the dimension of behavior), is more likely to produce the changes we want. For example, Lynn became very upset when Gary became attracted to another woman and was considering becoming more deeply involved with her. Lynn was aware of her hurt while maintaining respect for his choices. She expressed her hurt and allowed herself to cry without being accusatory or demanding, although she reserved the option to move out in case she needed to take care of herself in this way.

Gary was touched by her vulnerable sharing and appreciated not being criticized or told that he was acting immaturely or insensitively – invalidating accusations that had hurt him in previous relationships. Allowing himself to be affected by her hurt, he experienced a shift from being confused about what to do to feeling a deeper sense of intimacy with her. Lynn also discovered that expressing her real feelings produced an outcome in which she felt closer to Gary. Interestingly, it is this feeling of closeness that each of them had really been wanting, and which never would have resulted had she tried to make him feel guilty or change his behavior in some coercive way. It is likely that he would have then simply rebelled against the threat to his autonomy. In other words, her willingness to be vulnerable (and not controlling) had a surprisingly powerful effect that, indirectly, led to the deeper commitment she had been wanting.

Self-revealing statements create a climate in which it is vastly easier for another to remain attentive and interested in what we are saying. Reflecting an open-handed approach, they act as a gesture of goodwill and trust. Rather than condemn, insult, or defy, they open a door through which our real selves can be seen and empathetically understood. Consequently, conflicts or differences can be more easily resolved because the other is invited to visit and participate in our inner world of feelings and meanings.

Intrusive statements are almost always experienced as hurtful, even though we might like to perceive ourselves as having our reactions under control. In actuality, our natural organismic response (however enlightened we may think we are), is one of 'fight or flight'. Unless our inner caretaker is highly developed, we will tend to attack the other to show that he or she is wrong or less than respectable in some way. Or, we will withdraw in order to escape feeling hurt. Attacking or withdrawing are opposite ways of dealing with our fear or terror. Becoming verbally aggressive, our bodies rigidify as we contract internally and prepare ourselves for a battle. Retreating from the struggle, tensions subside (at least temporarily) as we hope to return to some sense of inner equilibrium. Whether we withdraw or attack, the more subtle dimensions of felt experience become lost and the possibility for open communication becomes more remote.

Unfortunately, the act of attacking or withdrawing only serves to further remove us from the very place within ourselves where we need to reside in order to experience the contact and intimacy we want. In reality, it is not far away. As human beings we possess the unique capacity to discover a serene territory that exists somewhere beneath the biologically programmed 'fight or flight' response. The key to that territory lies in our capacity to simply experience the threatening feelings that exist immediately prior to our impulse to attack or flee. The major ones, as we have been mentioning throughout, are fear (or terror), sadness (or grief), hurt (or woundedness), anger (or rage), embarrassment (or shame), loneliness (or isolation), and longing (or intense desire). Personal growth is largely a function of our capacity to be with these feelings in an accepting, sensitive manner. The goal is to befriend them, not transcend them.

The ability to be a caretaker for ourselves in regard to these feelings – that is, to simply be with them in an allowing way, can have a surprisingly transformative effect upon our lives and relationships. When we become capable of welcoming and being with these feelings as they arise within ourselves, our hearts and minds can remain open as we experience difficulties in relation to another person. As we face the 'demons' (scary unwanted feelings) within ourselves and communicate these feelings to another, an interesting thing tends to happen. Being with and sharing intense feelings with another person are two essential ways of moving toward a deep place of restful contact within ourselves and in relation to another being. As we learn to stabilize in our capacity to identify and be present to a full range of human feelings, we become more and more at home with ourselves. From this base we can then openly communicate our experience to another person. Doing so, we come to know and understand one another more deeply. Communication becomes the bridge between our two separate worlds.

Those moments during which basic emotions, insistent needs, and personal concerns and dissatisfactions are no longer coursing through us are rare ones. However, these quiet moments are often the most rich and meaningful ones of our lives. We sometimes experience this after a poignant sharing of threatening or tender feelings. Engaging one another in a real, honest manner, we may find that communication at times, progresses into a non-verbal sense of contact or intimacy that can be referred to as a state of union or an experience of love. Free of unsettling feelings or undercurrents of dissatisfaction, we simply become present with one another – two beings free of struggle and pretensions, simply breathing and being together.

The life process involves a natural ebb and flow of experiencing emotions (sometimes disturbing, sometimes pleasant), communicating them as we are moved to do so, and simply being joyfully present within ourselves, or in relation to one another – wordlessly and wholeheartedly. By not resisting any of these states as they happen to arise, we allow them to take their natural course. The overall direction is toward ever greater happiness, well-being, freedom, and aliveness. The means of getting there is to welcome whatever experiences come to us and develop a caring relationship with them so that positive changes may occur. The way to accelerate our development in this direction is to find at least one other person who wants to grow with us in this way – that is, someone who wants to know and befriend himself or herself more and more fully and learn to communicate with ever greater clarity, sensitivity, and openness.

As we commit ourselves to this new approach and find others to play and learn with, we may begin to discover the love, intimacy, and happiness we had previously tried to achieve by pushing aside painful feelings. As we become increasingly friendly with our feelings (that is, with ourselves), we become less and less confused and more and more in touch with who we are. As a result, we grow with fewer and fewer encumbrances toward an increasing sense of intimacy with ourselves, other people, and life itself.

CHAPTER 10
A guide to effective communication

It is usually obvious when you are feeling upset or unhappy in relation to another. What is frequently not so obvious is the real object of your dissatisfaction and what it is truly about. Acknowledging and getting in touch with your discontent can become an important doorway toward a deeper, more meaningful level of felt experience and connection with others. By availing yourself of the Focusing process, you can make progressive movement from the surface level of your initial felt reaction to a deeper realm of what you are really feeling and wanting. In this manner, the spirit of Focusing may help you touch your essential experience as a prelude to formulating concise, congruent communications that can diffuse conflicts, enhance mutual understanding, and encourage intimacy.

We will now present a specific three-step model through which you can learn to deliver effective, self-revealing communications. Understanding and using these guidelines will increase the possibilities of enjoying non-coercive conflict resolution and the growth of trust and loving contact in your relationships.

The three aspects of communication that we will discuss are:

1   Identifying and non-critically expressing to the other person the specific action that has triggered your upset or dissatisfaction.[1]
2   Expressing your resulting felt experience as accurately and succinctly as possible.
3   Requesting what you need or want in order to feel more nourished or loved by the other person.

Step 1 describes the words, behavior, or act of omission that has led to your displeasure. It is helpful to be as specific as

possible so the other person will understand what you are referring to. It is also beneficial to be as concise as possible so that
you do not overwhelm the person with unnecessary verbiage or
lengthy explanations that can obscure your main message.

Being descriptive rather than evaluative of another's behavior
is more likely to produce welcome changes. Evaluations and
judgments typically provoke antagonism, misunderstanding, and
defensiveness. Stating an observation as objectively and 'cleanly'
as possible makes it easier for the other person to hear us
and respond favorably to us. Descriptions that are interpretive,
biased, or blaming tend to be threatening to another's self-
esteem and are therefore usually resented or opposed. For
example, a person may wisely resist an accusatory statement
such as, 'When you don't care enough to call me when you're
late, I feel annoyed.' This statement includes the judgment and
untested assumption that he or she does not care about us. We
are unfairly equating 'not calling' with 'not caring.' Even if this
were true, we are more likely to be heard and to create a safe
atmosphere for a non-defensive response if we can formulate a
statement such as 'When you didn't call to tell me you'd be late,
I felt annoyed. I also felt sad as I imagined that you didn't really
care about me.' Referring to the fact that he or she did not
call is an objective, indisputable description of the behavior of
concern. And saying, 'I *imagined* you didn't care about me'
clearly demonstrates that we are appropriately owning our
assumption as *our* assumption. Insisting that our supposition is
the absolute truth leaves little room for discussion or resolution.
Voicing a concern in a tentative manner invites a thoughtful
response or clarifying dialogue.

Evaluative or vaguely defined statements are difficult to
respond to because a person may feel attacked, pigeonholed, or
perplexed regarding what we mean. For instance, the assertion,
'When you get stubborn and defensive, I feel frustrated' is not
a description of an observed behavior, but is rather a judgmental
analysis of their behavior. Rephrasing this statement to reflect
our actual observation, we might say, 'When you respond very
quickly to a concern I have about our relationship, I feel
frustrated.'

On those occasions when you are uncertain about what is
really troubling you, it may be helpful to spend some time

Focusing on the matter. Penetrating to the heart of what is bothering you and then expressing your central concern can minimize frustrations resulting from unproductive discussions or arguments about tangential issues. For example, you may feel upset when your partner or friend talks about other men. You may profit by taking some time to consult with your bodily felt sense to check whether this is really what is agitating you. Exploring this internally, you may suddenly realize that you actually feel upset only when she talks about Bob. That's it! Hearing about other friends is fine, but there is something about the way she talks about Bob that agitates you.

Step 1 provides an important foundation for the rest of the communication process. Being unclear about what triggers strong reactions inside us, our further communications are likely to be muddled and ineffective. Based upon a pseudo concern, or a minor aspect of a more fundamental concern, we remain bewildered and may produce confusion or mistrust in the other person. Instead of barking up the wrong tree, we can be more effective by taking some quiet time to notice what is really getting in the way of feeling good in relation to another person.

It is often helpful to remember the basic Focusing guideline that even when you feel pressured to produce instant answers, you need *not* be perfectly clear immediately. Such critical demands, whether internally or externally imposed, tend to increase anxiety, diminish self-worth, and generate confusion that further clouds the issue. Unable to tolerate uncertainty, you may succumb to these performance pressures and blurt out the first response that comes to mind. Doing so can quickly lead down a blind alley. Communication can be more productive if you take the time necessary to become clear about what you are experiencing. At first, you may have only a limited grasp of what is happening for you. After some Focusing, you may become clearer and can then express yourself better, even if tentatively. Sometime later, you may experience the matter even more vividly, and can then communicate further.

It may be advantageous to spend preliminary time Focusing alone so that you have some understanding of what is bothering you before presenting a concern to your friend or spouse. This can give you a head start on defining the specific behavior of concern and subsequent feelings triggered in you. Communicating the furthest step you have taken through self-reflection with this issue can accelerate the process of resolution.

The second step of the communication process involves contacting your bodily felt experience. As you sense what is occurring inside yourself, some preliminary feelings that are vague or fuzzy may begin to surface. Being with your bodily felt experience of an unclear feeling can lead to a natural process whereby deeper feelings supersede initial ones. As underlying experience becomes more apparent, liberating perspectives may emerge.

For example, you may, at first, feel angry whenever your friend talks about Bob. A typical reaction is either to stifle the anger (with associated critical beliefs that you are being silly, immature, or overly concerned), or express it and hope for some kind of quick change in the other's behavior. An alternate approach, consistent with the spirit of Focusing, is to stay with the experience of the anger – that is, allow it to be and simply feel it, without necessarily expressing it. Being with your bodily experience of anger, without jumping to any conclusions about what it means, you may notice the emergence of a previously unrecognized feeling, such as fear. A word such as 'threatened' may then arise out of your bodily felt sense.

You may continue Focusing for as many cycles as you like, either alone, or, if you care to take the risk, in the company of your friend. Deciding to Focus further, you remain with the bodily felt sense of being threatened. Perhaps there is a jumpiness in your stomach or a shakiness throughout your entire body. Then, after a few minutes of quietly sitting with the whole sense of feeling threatened, you may ask a question that invites a felt meaning to arise – that is, a sense of what this feeling of being threatened is really about.

Exploring the meaning of your feelings is an optional part of Step 2. It is often sufficiently effective and clarifying to simply experience and assert your feelings. At other times, communicating the meaning of these feelings can lead to deeper resolution. Remaining attuned to your bodily felt sense, you may ask an open-ended question such as, 'What is so threatening about her mentioning Bob?' You can then patiently wait for some new response to emerge from within. For instance, it may occur that you are afraid of being left behind; you dread that painfully familiar sense of abandonment that has befallen you in the past – one that you were unable to effectively deal with at that time.

Identifying and understanding your feelings, you are in a better position to communicate them in a profoundly simple and meaningful way. Steps 1 and 2 may then be formulated as follows: 'When you talk about Bob, I feel threatened; I am afraid you may leave me.' You are then ready for Step 3: an active expression of your needs or preferences.

Beneath each of our judgments, criticisms, and resentments lies an unfulfilled need or want. We are more likely to satisfy these needs if we can discover and directly ask for what we want. Unwilling to do so, we may succumb to complaining about our fate, blaming others for their insensitivity, or becoming apathetic toward life. Although there are obviously no guarantees that we will receive what we want, we are much more likely to have needs and preferences met if we can learn to ask in a spirit of courageous vulnerability. Crippled by shame, embarrassment, or a fear of recurring rejection, we are prone to live guarded, frustrated lives. Scared to express our needs and resentful that they are not being met, we become strangers to one another, sadly isolated and undernourished.

Through Focusing, our needs can become progressively clearer. If they are initially vague, we may express them as best we can. As we Focus further, or through a spontaneous realization between Focusing sessions, our wants may become more tangible. As they do, or as our needs change, we can communicate these. Growth involves a lifelong process of change. Keeping abreast of our changing needs supports this growth.

Continuing the earlier example, moving to part 3 of the communication process, you may ask yourself a question such as, 'What am I missing here?' or 'Is there something I want from her?' or 'What do I need in order to breathe a little easier about all of this?' Whatever arises can be checked with your bodily felt sense. Does that say it? If it does not quite fit, can you notice what you actually need in order to feel more nourished or cared for in this relationship? Perhaps, for example, you would like your friend not to talk about Bob anymore. Or, you may ask her to see him less often. Another possible discovery is that you need to understand why she likes seeing him, or which of her needs are being met that are not being met by you. Or, you may simply want some reassurance that she still loves you and wants to be with you.

Adding the third step to this communication process, we may state the following: 'When you talk about Bob, I feel threatened and I am afraid you may leave me. I need to know that you love me and that you are committed to working things through with me.' Such a clear, succinct communication invites a clear response from her felt experience. Feeling unthreatened, she may be moved to give you what you want. If she does not feel so inclined, she has an opportunity to explore whatever obstacles may be getting in her way, and express her own feelings and needs in a self-revealing manner. A continuing dialogue in this fashion may clarify the central issues that need resolution. This can lead to new understandings of one another, and increased feelings of love and intimacy as you touch the depths of each other's fears and aspirations. Or, differences may be exposed that cannot be easily resolved. This outcome may indicate a need for further discussion or a need for a professional therapist or counselor who can assist you and your partner to become clearer about how you feel, what you want, and how each of you may be contributing to the conflict. Working these issues through may lead to reconciliation through unexpected avenues. Or, if the differences are found to be too great, both of you can learn more about yourselves so that subsequent relationships may be more enduring and rewarding.

This three-step process may feel awkward and unnatural at first, especially while trying to communicate in a new way during emotionally charged times. However, with consistent attention, steady practice, gentle caring, and reliable feedback from those with whom you practice, this manner of expression can become a more natural part of your life.

At those times when your feelings are not readily accessible or when you are particularly stuck or confused, you may want to pursue a more informal and lengthy discussion with your partner or friend. 'Talking it out' is sometimes beneficial in order to become clearer about your central feelings and needs. This may help free up energies and safeguard you from trying too hard or becoming self-critical during those occasions when this process becomes difficult to use. Conversing informally may then lead to the issues that are the most emotionally charged or in need of attention.

We will now present some sample statements that illustrate various ways in which this communication process may be successfully used, and common ways in which it can be misused or distorted.

SKILLFUL COMMUNICATION: When you call me stupid I feel hurt; I'd like you to stop calling me that; I want to feel more respect from you.

UNSKILLFUL COMMUNICATION: When you pick on me, it drives me crazy. I want you to get off my case!

This communication is ineffective because it accuses the other person of picking on you. This interpretation may or may not be accurate. Even if correct, it will tend to elicit a defensive response because it is a critical statement. Also, to add 'it drives me crazy,' is a vague remark that neglects to disclose any specific feeling. Taking some time to be with your felt response, you may notice a feeling such as anger, hurt, sadness, or embarrassment. You can then express the main feeling (or a combination of them), rather than respond in a way that is confusing or inflammatory. Part three of the above statement, 'I want you to get off my case,' is an angry or hostile statement. Instead of expressing this anger in a hostile way, it may be expressed more 'cleanly' and directly in part two of the communication process by simply stating that you feel angry when you are called 'stupid'.

SKILLFUL STATEMENT: When you straightened out my collar at the party I felt embarrassed. It reminded me of what my mother did when I was a kid. I'd appreciate it if you wouldn't do that in front of other people, but rather tell me about it later.

UNSKILLFUL COMMUNICATION: When you treated me like a child at the party, I felt like socking you. If you ever do that again, I won't go to another party with you. I need you to cut that out!

There is an assumption here that you were treated like a child. In reality, the other person may not have viewed you as a child.

It is less presumptuous and more self-revealing to disclose that the feelings triggered by his or her behavior were similar to unpleasant past experiences with your mother. Sharing this meaning may help another person to empathize with you more readily.

The statement, 'I felt like socking you,' may be amusing if it is spoken playfully and if expressed to someone who knows you well enough to appreciate your colorful humor. However, it may also be received as a hostile statement and therefore is best stated in a more direct, 'clean' way.

Threatening not to go to any more parties may provide some kind of satisfaction, but it can easily undermine trust and generate an escalation of resentment and defensiveness. You may find it equally satisfying to state your anger openly or be angry in a non-attacking, non-vengeful way. There is then a greater likelihood to preserve trust and achieve resolution.

The last statement, 'I need you to cut that out!' is an attack or a demeaning injunction. It is reminiscent of the critical, hurtful statements that may have injured us in the past. If you have a strong emotional charge regarding a particular issue, you may want to spend some time processing it (either alone, with your friend, or with an uninvolved third party) until you feel some release of the charge. You may then be able to express what you need more clearly and effectively.

SKILLFUL STATEMENT: I felt angry when you left the house during our discussion. I need to sit down with you and talk more about how I'm feeling about our relationship.

UNSKILLFUL COMMUNICATION: When you run away from our discussions, I feel that there's no hope for our relationship. I need you to face reality instead of withdrawing from me and avoiding your feelings.

It is more objective and less evaluative simply to state the fact that he or she left the house. Omitting the emotionally loaded assumption that he or she was running away may afford you a more receptive hearing. Also, stating that there is no hope for the relationship is an opinion or idea, not a feeling. The actual feeling may be one of hopelessness or sadness. If so, you can simply state this feeling and then allow additional feelings or felt meanings to arise from that.

Asserting that, 'I need you to face reality,' is not a self-disclosing 'I statement.' A more self-revealing remark would be, 'I need to have my feelings honored, or 'I need to have more communication with you about our relationship.' Accusing the person of withdrawing or avoiding feelings is a judgment or analysis that may further hamper communication, even if there is some truth to your perception. Your friend will probably feel uncomfortable with your habit of analyzing him or her, or diagnosing what *you* think is his or her problem or the interpersonal difficulty.

SKILLFUL COMMUNICATION: When you say that my desire to spend more time with friends is unreasonable, I feel angry. I want my choices to be respected.

UNSKILLFUL COMMUNICATION: I don't like it when you try to tell me what to do. I need to do what feels right for me.

The general statement, 'I don't like it,' does not reveal much about how you really feel. Also, the other person may not necessarily be telling you what to do. Even if he or she is trying to tell you what to do, stating this may be provoking. It is more skillful and less antagonistic to repeat back as accurately as possible the precise words that have led to your feeling of frustration or anger.

Stating that, 'I need to do what feels right for me,' is a positive, caretaking stance. However, it fails to make a request that may lead to more nurturing or intimacy. Caretaking statements inclusive of the other person would be ones such as, 'I'd appreciate it if you honored my desire to enjoy other people's companionship when I want to do so.'

Expressing feelings does not necessarily mean that we will be heard. Asking for what we want does not always mean we will receive it. However, communicating in a non-judgmental, self-revealing manner that accurately reflects our felt experience gives us the greatest possibility for mutually satisfying outcomes.

EXPLORING HIDDEN AGENDAS

Unproductive discussions often occur when we are narrowly focused upon a specific outcome. Communicating for the sole sake of getting what we want often backfires because it is blind to exploring alternative resolutions palatable to both parties. Also, maintaining a hidden agenda is detrimental to communication because it reflects an unwillingness to trust the other to respond sensitively and fairly if we place all of our cards on the table. A lasting resolution to a difficult issue is more likely to occur as we enter in good faith into an open-minded, open-ended process of communication. Relinquishing the pursuit of a specific outcome and remaining open to a changing array of feelings, meanings, and needs within ourselves and in the other person, we may be surprised to discover an unexpected resolution.

For example, Jeffrey was upset because Lois was planning a ten-day trip out of town to visit her parents. Ordinarily, Jeffrey would react either by trying to convince her to stay, by venting his resentment in covert, vengeful ways (such as by ignoring her or staying out late), or by attempting to manipulate her into feeling guilty through pouting. Experimenting with a new approach, he communicated in a self-revealing way, saying, 'I feel very sad that you're going away. I'll miss you.' Sensing his vulnerability and uncharacteristic softness of expression, she was touched, and responded, 'I can really understand that; I feel some sadness too. I'm happy that you like being with me.' This tender interaction led to a rich moment of contact. Although she reaffirmed her decision to visit her parents because it was important to her, the process of trust-promoting communication changed how they felt toward one another. In other words, her actions did not change, but each of *them* changed through the delicate process of openly sharing feelings with one another. It is this dimension of change that most of us really want because it leads to the stronger sense of love and contact that is so nourishing to our being.

CRITICAL COMMUNICATIONS

Conflicts can remain unresolved or escalate when non-verbal cues such as tone of voice convey blame or ridicule, even though we formulate an impeccably non-judgmental communication. The spirit of our expression can override our best efforts to communicate using non-intrusive language. If such is the case, we would do well to expose the feelings and unmet needs that underlie our verbal or non-verbal communications. These can then be directly expressed.

Our best attempts to express feelings are sometimes distorted due to the contaminating influence of a tenacious inner critic. This makes it difficult to sort out our genuinely felt experience from socially conditioned feelings or wants. Rather than being organismically felt, some of our feelings may actually be created by a conditioned set of moralistic judgments, rigid opinions, or critical evaluations based upon socially taught beliefs regarding what is right or wrong, good or bad. Albert Ellis (1975) has created an entire system of psychotherapy (Rational-Emotive therapy) based upon the idea that many of our feelings derive from irrational or limited beliefs about reality. Intense emotions may sometimes be diffused by noticing if the perfectionistic demands of our inner critic are creating our feelings or fueling our upset. For example, through believing that it is absolutely important to be on time, we may be extremely upset when others are late. If we discern that our critical beliefs are responsible for generating these feelings, then we can learn to suspend our internal and external criticism as we become gentler with ourselves and others.

In another scenario, we may alternate between feeling furious and helpless because our intimate friend refuses to discuss the difficulties we are experiencing in our relationship. Failing to make progress through dialogue, we may explore how we are contributing to our own anguish. By doing so, we may realize that we are being influenced by the suppressive idea that we must remain with this one individual, who is viewed as our only possible source of love and nurturing.

Our feelings may also be controlled by the idea that if our relationship ends, it must do so on friendly terms since, after all, lovers 'should' remain friends. However, if we do not really feel drawn to remain friends, then submitting to the designs of our critical minds sets us up for continuing misery. It is therefore important to identify and relinquish unrealistic, critical beliefs that are adding to our upset or confusion. Doing so will help us discriminate our actual felt experience from conditioned feelings induced by our inner critic.

Communication need not be limited to problem-solving or conflict resolution. Intimacy and trust can also grow by expressing appreciation for a person's actions or for personal qualities that nurture us. Such a simple acknowledgment is a generous and often neglected way to express love and caring.

CHECKING OUT ASSUMPTIONS

A common and often unavoidable human tendency is to hold assumptions regarding other people. Through hearing someone's comments or observing a person's behavior, we often assume or imagine things that may be totally inaccurate. For example, if our friend is late to meet us at a concert we may assume that she is irresponsible or does not care about us. Or if we meet someone at a party who begins talking to a newly arrived friend, we may assume he is not interested in us.

Assumptions usually involve judgments or premature opinions such as, 'I think he's very selfish,' or 'I suspect she's angry with me.' They can also involve self-discounting thoughts, such as, 'He probably doesn't find me very interesting.' A curious fact is that we can live our entire lives based upon a set of untested assumptions. Checking them out requires that we become aware of what they are, followed by an act of courage to risk knowing the truth.

One way of dealing with our real or imaginary assumptions is through the simple act of observing them and 'letting them go.' In our experience, however, we have observed that 'letting go' is not as easy as it sounds. Assumptions and judgments tend to be very tenacious; they have a subtle way of lodging themselves in our minds, thus clouding our perception of things as they really are. We may *think* we have 'let go' when actually they have gone underground.

Gently checking out our assumptions is sometimes a more

effective way to 'let go' of them, as well as to feel closer to the other person. For example, if we have felt some distance from our spouse and hold the assumption that he or she is angry with us, we can check that out. If so, we can discuss what this is about, perhaps resolving a conflict that has been getting in the way of feeling good about the relationship.

When testing an assumption, it is often best to begin by getting permission to check them out. You can ask, for example, 'I'd like to check something out with you – is that okay?' Then proceed to test your assumption through one of a number of possible questions. For instance, you might say, 'I have an assumption that you are angry with me, is that right?' Or, 'I imagine that you are angry with me, is that true?' Or, simply, 'I've been wondering whether you've been angry with me lately.'

Airing assumptions is a way to get them off your chest. It also presents an opportunity for the other person to explore feelings or issues that may not have been obvious. Perhaps, for example, he or she is not feeling angry with you, but has been experiencing frustration at work. In this instance, you are indeed sensing some kind of upset, but it is not directed toward you.

Testing assumptions is generally more productive after a round or two of communicating your feelings, using the three communication steps described earlier. This may safeguard you from using it as a substitute for sharing your own vulnerable feelings. It is often easier to point out what you think is happening inside another's inner world than it is to understand your own. Sloppily used, checking out assumptions can degenerate into pointing out the assumed faults of the other person, as by saying, 'I think you're very insecure, don't you see what I'm talking about?' Or, 'You're such a nag – just like your mother! Why don't you admit it!' These critical, if not hostile, communications undermine trust.

Testing assumptions is best done through a gentle tone of questioning or wondering, as in the statement, 'I may be off the mark, but it seems to me that you feel very threatened whenever I see a male friend – is that so?' An assumption such as this can be shared with a sense of caring and compassion, rather than with condescension or resentment. If you proceed in a gentle manner, the other person will be more likely to listen to an observation that may expose a deeper level of vulnerability.

While we are sometimes totally inaccurate in our perceptions, at other times we have clear insight into other people's private world. While this is traditionally the domain of therapists and counselors, we can occasionally play a meaningful role as teachers for each other. Of course, we need to be careful not to go too far and intrude upon territory where we are not welcome. But we can, in a limited way, facilitate each other's growth by *being there* for one another as we sensitively check out our assumptions.

For example, you may express an assumption that your friend sometimes seems insecure. If your friend acknowledges this, an inner release may occur for you simply by observing him or her owning that experience more directly. And your friend may feel safer and more intimate with you knowing that you accept and love him or her even with this trait.

Just as loving ourselves means fully accepting ourselves, so does feeling loved by another help us feel accepted and loved as the less than perfect beings we are. And, somehow, it is easier to love others when they acknowledge their limitations and human shortcomings, rather than struggle to hide them or pretend they do not exist. Being real with one another creates a climate most conducive to growth-promoting dialogue.

It is unwise and usually counterproductive to share our assumptions unless some foundation of trust exists. But even in relationships where considerable trust has developed, it is important to state assumptions in an unpretentious, tentative manner. Using words such as 'I imagine,' 'I fantasize,' or 'I wonder' conveys a humble awareness that we may be misperceiving what is actually true.

We often see others through the filter of our own fears, worries, and needs. As such, our perceptions and assumptions are often off the mark. This fact can be recognized by observing married couples who are emotional strangers to one another. Firmly holding false assumptions regarding the nature of another's feelings, needs, motivations, or character, we rob ourselves of an opportunity for resolution. Getting these out in the open can free us from their tendency to stifle intimacy.

If you remain convinced that your assumption is correct, even if denied by a person, your wisest course is to suspend this assumption and return to a self-revealing expression of your feelings and needs. Insisting that you are right or maintaining some judgment or conviction about a person will never lead to the love and intimacy you want. Many people go to their graves being 'right,' but utterly unhappy.

CHAPTER 11
Working with anger

Anger is a powerful, yet little understood human emotion. Our inability to deal with it effectively is a frequent cause of problems in our relationships. A major factor that contributes to this difficulty is the common misconception that anger is somehow 'bad', destructive, or inappropriate. It is true that the way in which resentments are expressed can lead to a great deal of hurt in relationships and violence in the world. However, it would be a grave error to conclude that anger, in itself, is responsible for the destructiveness, and should therefore be avoided.

Rather than maintain a simplistic good/bad perception of anger, it is more useful to adopt a non-judgmental attitude toward it. If it is true that growth involves learning to love ourselves, then it follows that we must learn to fully accept ourselves, including our anger. The unfortunate alternative is to turn the anger inward against ourselves. In other words, unacknowledged and unexpressed anger gets held in the body, creating tension that may be experienced as frustration or anxiety. Or, when resentments have no healthy outlet, our bodily held anger may be felt as a chronic fatigue or depression – the anger turns against us, suppressing our energy and vitality. Internalized anger may also be partially responsible for those times when we feel confused – resentments fuse with other emotions and unproductive thoughts that then overwhelm us.

Bottled-up anger can also lead to physical symptoms such as headaches, ulcers, and an array of other illnesses whose causes we are only beginning to understand. In the years ahead, we may recognize that an accumulation of unacknowledged anger coupled with an inability to deal with it responsibly contributes significantly to the origin of many common diseases.

A key to our physical as well as emotional well-being involves allowing the experience of anger to simply be, without either judging it or trying to get rid of it due to our fear or aversion. Opening to our anger can then become a way to unlock suppressed energy and vitality. Dealing with it responsibly can enliven our relationships and rejuvenate those that have become stagnant or boringly comfortable.

Once we accept anger as a neutral energy, rather than morally judge it, we are in a position to differentiate between its responsible expression, and the impulse to vent it in destructive, hurtful ways. The need to communicate it in healthy ways becomes particularly obvious once we realize that we cannot *not* express our anger. There is some kind of inner intelligence within our organism that wants to express it. This healthy urge manifests in unhealthy, indirect ways when our belief system does not permit a direct experience of the anger.

It is the indirect expression of anger that has harmful, insidious effects upon relationships. Psychologists call this 'passive-aggressive' behavior because, instead of expressing the anger or communicating about it, we act it out in passive ways. For example, if we fear the consequences of sharing our resentment directly, we may express anger indirectly by missing appointments, arriving late, withholding affection, or acting in a variety of spiteful ways. One client, for instance, stated that she took great satisfaction in running up her husband's charge accounts. At the time, she was not even aware of her anger, but upon closer exploration of her motives, she realized what she was actually feeling. She had experienced some relief (a re-emergence of her sense of power) by 'getting back' at her husband for not giving her the caring and affection she wanted. But the relationship suffered because the anger did not have a chance to be expressed openly and explored in terms of its deeper meaning. Once the wisdom of the anger was understood, some resolution occurred as she became more willing to express her need for affection.

While some people disguise their anger through its passive expression, others vent it in an exaggerated fashion through unpredictable explosions. We sometimes read stories about the 'nice guy' on the block who kills his wife and children. While the neighbors are left puzzled, it is no wonder to those who know that when resentments are repressed, they go underground and amass greater force for a future eruption. This pattern is familiar in relationships where one has a self-image of not being an angry person. For example, one individual who was deeply involved with spiritual practices had a strong conviction that it was wrong to get angry. One day, however, she exploded in a fierce rage. Being uncomfortable with her anger, she tried to cover it up by being sweet and forgiving. But, as inevitably occurs when anger is submerged, her fury erupted despite her best efforts to keep it under control.

Once we can acknowledge and feel our anger, we can begin to differentiate between its responsible expression and the impulse to vent it in destructive ways. It is not the anger that hurts others, but rather the blaming, judgmental ways in which it is often communicated. Gaining greater control over our anger does not mean suppressing it, but rather learning how to channel it in a way that can lead to greater intimacy and communication.

LEARNING TO EXPRESS 'CLEAN' ANGER

The expression of anger can be distinguished by whether it is 'clean' or 'destructive'. Destructive anger is very hurtful because it is tinged with personality attacks or judgmental criticisms. For example, through choice of words, tone of voice, or movements of the body, we may convey a message such as 'You're pretty stupid,' or 'you're really selfish,' or 'you're wrong, don't you know anything!?' These and similar invalidating communications constitute an attack on the other person. They say, in effect, 'You are not a worthwhile human being; you do not deserve love and respect.' Such messages are especially hurtful because they reinforce the bad feelings we may already have about ourselves.

Receiving hurtful communications from another, we instinctively protect ourselves by either attacking or withdrawing. We may withdraw in a number of ways, such as by watching television, compulsively eating, drinking, going to sleep, refusing to talk, or threatening to end the relationship. Or, rather than withdrawing, we may retaliate by blaming or verbally attacking the other – becoming self-righteous and mentally deciding that the other person is wrong, bad, selfish, or immature. This leads to a spiraling escalation of tensions. Whether we withdraw or attack, the relationship suffers because one or both parties are left feeling hurt, defensive, or isolated. Surprisingly, this toxic pattern can continue indefinitely, leading to a painful negativity toward relationships and bitterness toward life.

Clean anger, on the other hand, does not focus on making the other person wrong for their behavior, feelings, or opinions. Instead of blaming or analyzing the other person ('you're too needy' or 'you're so depressed!'), or assuming to know their motives ('you're just trying to get back at me,' or 'you only care about yourself!'), a clean communication reveals one's own feelings and unmet needs, uncontaminated by blame or guilt-producing statements. For example, clean anger could be expressed in the following manner: 'I'm angry about these dishes in the sink!' Included in this communication may be an emotional intensity in one's voice, but it is clean because the individual is merely expressing his or her feeling without implying (through words, tone of voice, or gestures) that the other person is wrong or suspect in some way. In contrast, a destructive communication would involve saying something like, 'How many times do I have to tell you not to leave your dirty dishes in the sink!' At first, the distinction may appear to be a subtle one, but there is a crucial difference. Receiving the clean expression of anger, we hear, 'This person is angry about dishes in the sink.' Since we do not feel attacked, we may feel inclined to respond in an accommodating way. In the destructive communication, we feel nagged at and hear, 'I'm bad for doing something wrong.' As a result, we may withdraw in order to remove ourselves from a hurtful situation. Or we may give voice to our anger through an ineffectual, sarcastic remark such as, 'Yes, dear,' or 'There you go complaining again. . . .'

Feeling entitled to experience anger and express it in a clean, self-revealing way provides a direct, psychologically healthy outlet for it. As a result, there is less of a tendency for it to leap out later in irrational, hurtful ways (whether passively or actively). Our anger, plus other issues surrounding it, have a greater chance of being resolved through a simple, guiltless expression in the moment. Daniel Wile, a couples therapist, describes this clearly:

> An angry feeling or impulse, experienced and expressed in
> a direct and straightforward manner, often has a clarifying
> and beneficial effect. . . when anger is warded off, it
> reappears in regressive forms, as sudden rage, sadistic fant-
> asies, or chronic irritability. If fear or self-criticism (guilt)
> prevent people from being assertive, the impulse goes
> underground and re-emerges in sudden blatant expressions
> (aggression) or subdued, inhibited ones (nonassertion).[1]

In addition, by releasing anger, our genuine love for the other
can continue to grow, rather than be smothered by ever-
increasing layers of resentment.

A clean expression of anger reflects the understanding that
others do not cause our feelings. The common statement, 'You
make me so angry,' depicts how anger is often blamed on the
one toward whom we feel it. While another's words or actions
can certainly bring up our anger, the other person cannot be
held fully responsible for it. Our present upset is often the result
of many factors, such as our unmet need for love, a re-stimulation
of unresolved past hurts, feelings of unworthiness, fears of rejection, as well as the present anger-provoking situation. Our
present feeling cannot be reduced simply to past causes or only
to the present circumstance. Rather, our feeling is usually created
by both. Growth comes through honoring our emotion as it
arises, expressing it cleanly, and exploring it further internally
if it seems particularly charged or out of proportion to the
current situation.

The expression of anger need not be seen as threatening when
expressed responsibly. In effect, it states, 'I do not like this!' or
'I won't accept that!' Anger sends a big 'No!' message to the
other: 'No! I won't stand for this!' Through our anger, we
stand up for ourselves, recover our self-esteem, and express our
unwillingness to be abused, ignored, or depreciated by another.
Even if we feel powerless to change the actual circumstances,
expressing our anger enables us to release bodily held frustrations and energies, which can lead to a welcome change of
attitude toward the situation. And, perhaps surprisingly, the
situation itself may change once we have dealt with our feelings
about it.

While it is important to be mindful of our felt experience, we are not suggesting that anger be expressed without regard for another's feelings or needs. As we grow more intimate with ourselves – becoming better acquainted with our true feelings and discovering patterns that no longer serve us – it becomes more possible to express ourselves while having an awareness of another's experience and a sensitivity to his or her feelings and well-being. Once the anger has subsided, we can demonstrate concern about the impact that our anger may have had by asking how the other person is feeling as a result of our communication. We can then be available to receive their response in a caring way.

One of the most difficult and challenging aspects of skillful communication is to integrate a sense of personal power with compassion – developing an ability to assert our own feelings and needs while maintaining a genuine caring for others. If we attend only to our own feelings, we become narcissistic. Preoccupied with ourselves, out of touch with the world around us, we feel disconnected from intimacy and therefore under-nourished in our very being. It is one of the great paradoxes of life that when we are focused only upon our own needs, they cannot possibly be fully met. On the other hand, if we pay exclusive attention to other people's feelings and reactions, we abandon our own genuine needs. This pattern may be reinforced by becoming identified with the self-image of being a compassionate or loving person. Seeing ourselves as more 'evolved' than others and obliged to care for them regardless of personal needs, we will again be left undernourished and disconnected from the interdependence that is natural to human existence. Eventually we may experience an angry outrage resulting from an accumulated sense of deprivation and self-neglect.

We grow up in a society that teaches us to conceal our anger. As a result, we hold it back, and may justify this through state-ments such as, 'I don't want to hurt him,' or 'I don't want her to feel badly.' What seems like a noble concern for protecting others is frequently a hidden fear of being disliked. The fear of rejection, and subsequent fear of feeling isolated and alone, is a major reason for withholding our anger and failing to be completely honest with one another. However, taking the risk to be authentic in this way can often lead to the growth of trust when we are relating to a person who appreciates such honesty.

Taking care of ourselves by expressing clean anger can be done in a variety of ways. 'Getting angry' without blame is the most intense way, as in shouting, 'I want to have a say in what movie we see tonight!' This vocal anger may be especially appropriate in situations where we have stifled resentments and felt unheard for a long time.

As we work with our anger and release some of the charge that may have been accumulating, we can eventually learn to stand up for ourselves without becoming irate. Becoming comfortable with our right to say 'no,' or to stand up for what we want, we can begin to embody an assertiveness that appropriately matches the situation. Doing so, we learn to simply state how we feel, what is bothering us, or what we want, untinged by leftover anger that we may still be carrying from the past.

Experiencing anger and learning to express it cleanly can lead to other important insights about ourselves. For instance, we may discover a sense of hurt or fear beneath a more obvious layer of resentment. For example, we may realize that just below the surface of our anger about the dishes not being washed, lies a deeper concern about whether we are really loved. In this case, our reactive anger is precariously sitting atop a storehouse of hurt of which we may only be vaguely aware. However, if anger is our most distinct feeling, then that is where we must begin to access our deeper level of experience. If we avoid the anger entirely (for example, by believing that we should just forgive and forget), then we may rob ourselves of a vital opportunity to follow the wisdom of our felt process to its natural outcome. As a result, we bypass a chance to learn more about ourselves and become more intimate with another person.

Expressing anger cleanly and non-defensively can place us in a vulnerable position in relation to the person with whom we are angry. In order to help us feel safer in beginning new patterns of behavior in a relationship, we may wish to agree to the basic ground rule that each person has permission to cleanly express anger. This implies a willingness to make clearer discrimination between clean and destructive anger. Perceiving this distinction is not always easy. Individuals with a commitment to their own growth and to one another's well-being can sensitively explore how to communicate their anger in ways that lead to a resolution of conflicts.

Another factor that can support productive communication concerns how we relate to others' anger. Can we simply receive it? Can we hear how they are feeling without counter-attacking or defending ourselves? We certainly have a right to respond, but can we first hear their feelings and point of view? Responding differs from reacting. Reactions tend to be automatic and habitual, and are often triggered by underlying fears, such as feeling unloved. Responding occurs after we have received their communication, allowed it to touch us in some way, and taken time to notice the fresh feelings and meanings that then arise within us. Can we hear them without assuming that it means something negative about ourselves, or that the person no longer loves us simply because they are feeling angry? The simple act of hearing others' resentments can go a long way toward resolving it. People feel better when they sense that their anger is heard rather than avoided, received rather than judged as being wrong or inappropriate. The process of receiving others' anger and opening to the meaning it holds for them can lead to a precious moment of interpersonal contact.

A relationship that has love and trust as its context can become stronger through its ability to accommodate a wide range of human emotions. If trust is tenuous or uncertain, a wave of anger can jeopardize it. However, as trust grows, then, instead of being a threat, anger can be seen as conveying a crucial message that is calling for attention. If we really care about another, then we want to hear his or her anger and understand what it is really all about. Perhaps, for example, we gradually discover that they are feeling misunderstood, unappreciated, or unloved.

Learning to acknowledge our anger and hold a healthy respect for the wisdom it contains is an important step toward the development of meaningful intimacy. The mutual sharing of anger in clean, self-revealing ways can lead to a process of communication that can help two individuals feel closer to one another. As normally suppressed energies are released and we more intimately touch one another, our relationships can flourish in unexpected ways.

CHAPTER 12

Toward a new perspective on commitment and marriage

The notion of commitment is one of the most perplexing aspects of intimate relationships. We will offer a new concept of commitment based upon an understanding of what best supports the growth of a deeply felt union. Our remarks are based upon the observation that those who are growing as human beings by opening to felt experience appear to undergo a significant shift in the nature and meaning of their commitments. Broadly speaking, this shift involves the transition from a 'formal commitment' to what we will refer to as a 'process commitment.'

A formal commitment is a pledge to an accepted conventional structure that is believed to be necessary to achieve respectability and happiness. Society cherishes such commitments because in previous times they were necessary for protection, security, and social order. This structure, however, is no longer essential for survival. While clinging to the old ways may offer some modicum of security, the love for which we truly hunger may never arise by conforming to such conventions.

A 'process commitment' is a more flexible, yet equally serious, commitment to the well-being of both ourselves and others. It reflects a consistent dedication to embody factors that reliably lead to personal growth, which provides a foundation for love and intimacy. A process commitment also involves the steady development of a genuinely felt caring and love for others. As we commit ourselves to a *process* of growing closer to ourselves and others, we may find ourselves actually experiencing the very thing that a 'heroic' formal commitment was supposed to guarantee. Let us now mention some popular formal commitments, and then discuss how a process commitment is a more viable means of enjoying the enduring sense of loving and being loved that we want.

One common formal commitment is the agreement always to love our partner. Such an assertion, however, is highly presumptuous and unrealistic. Love is a tender gift that ensues when conditions are supportive. We cannot *decide* to love another person through an act of will or some kind of gallant effort. Love and intimacy awaken in their own way and in their own time. They come into being as two individuals feel sufficiently trusting of each other, and when surrounding circumstances are conducive. Although we can be committed to creating an internal and external climate in which love and closeness are more likely to emerge and develop, we cannot make ourselves consistently feel a loving connection.

Another socially prized commitment is pledging a lifelong agreement to remain with a particular person – the traditional marriage vow. Again, however, it is highly questionable whether it is possible to sustain such a vow without sacrificing our integrity. This vow assumes that we can predict what will be best for us at a future time. In addition, such an agreement can easily lend itself to a variety of abuses that can both obstruct the personal call toward self-actualization and stifle the growth potential of the marriage.

One widespread abuse of the customary vow to remain together until 'death do us part' is that through the continual weight of such a formal commitment, we can easily forget that a central purpose of the relationship is to nurture both our growth as a person and the growth of our love for each other. Making a primary commitment to a lifelong partnership, rather than to supporting conditions under which love may flourish and spread to our children and other people, we insult the marriage by overlooking its real meaning. Clinging to a mate as an end in itself, or as a strategy to eliminate our fear of the unknown, may relieve loneliness and provide a semblance of security, but the price we pay is often one of betraying the precious calling toward the actualization of our full potential.

If our primary investment is in maintaining the permanence of the marriage, we may be inclined to hide feelings or bypass conflicts that are perceived as potential threats to marital stability. These conflicts, however, are vitally necessary to explore and resolve if marital love and intimacy are to endure and deepen. If, in fact, we protect ourselves and one another from feelings or concerns in order to hold on to the relationship, the dishonesty and withholding will themselves lead to the demise of a felt love and intimacy. Constrained by the notion that we must remain together, or that love means that we are obliged to protect one another from unsettling truths, we may avoid discomforting topics that could lead to difficulties.

The marital contract is frequently used to avoid growth, justify abuse, or deny responsibility for personal shortcomings that the marriage was somehow 'supposed to' alleviate. On the other hand, offering no substantive commitment would leave the relationship on shaky ground, subject to sudden dissolution at the earliest sign of emotional discomfort or conflict. How, then, can we find some safe middle ground that provides protection against the misuses of commitment, yet offers a supportive foundation for the continued growth of love and intimacy?

A useful direction may emerge as we begin to understand commitment to another person as something that gradually unfolds, beginning with a commitment to factors over which we have some degree of control.

THE BASIC COMMITMENT TO BE HONEST WITH OURSELVES AND OTHERS

Honesty is a factor that we have a considerable degree of control over; at any given moment, we can choose to conceal or reveal our actual feelings, perceptions, or intentions. The choice to be honest requires a related commitment to know and befriend ourselves more and more fully. It is this crucial commitment to ourselves — to grow as a person — that nourishes the ever-deepening rootedness from which trust and love can grow. Being devoted to discerning our real feelings, motives, and needs, plus a readiness to communicate these as congruently as possible, demonstrates a practical, though frequently overlooked, expression of our commitment to the growth of a relationship.

To express this in another way, reliable commitments to others must go hand in hand with a commitment to our own process of self-actualization. These two aspects of commitment are, in fact, inseparable. We cannot say 'yes' to another unless we are sufficiently in touch with our own depths. Otherwise, we are prone to make formal commitments from a place inside ourselves where we are mentally identified with intriguing images and empty beliefs, rather than genuine commitments that derive from being in touch with our felt experience. A real commitment is an ongoing process that must be renewed daily; it is not a 'once and for all' decision.

As you begin to open toward a more real, genuinely felt dimension of who you are as a person – that is, as you awaken to the deeper call of your being – you may realize, with some sadness, that the current circumstances of your life do not support your movement toward growth. More specifically, you may feel frustrated to discover that your present partner is not aligned with the direction of your life as you now see it unfolding before you. Recognizing such differences can provide an opportunity to expand the purpose and direction of the relationship if there is a mutual interest in doing so. Lacking a mutual intent to re-evaluate the premises underlying the relationship, you may need to consider separation in order to maintain the commitment to your own growth.

Having to choose between parting from your spouse or betraying the calling to become a more whole person is a painful decision. Departing can lead to much sadness and remorse resulting from having innocently misled another person, or from having been ignorant about your true needs. On the other hand, betraying yourself by remaining in an unsatisfying marriage may result in even more painful consequences. Your organism is likely to rebel emotionally or physically if you continue to live in opposition to genuine inner needs.

If you find yourself in such a situation, it is important to continue opening to your bodily felt experience in order to discover an appropriate direction. If separating feels like the better of two difficult choices, then, as you embody new learnings from this experience, you will be less likely to make a similar error in the future. Caring for yourself in an understanding and forgiving manner, and taking some time to grow within yourself, rather than diving too rapidly into a new relationship, will lead to more informed decisions regarding future involvements.

As we become committed to knowing and revealing how we

feel, what these feelings mean to us, and what we need in order to grow as a person, we then invite people into our world based upon a realistic view of who we are. Others can then freely choose to be with us or not. The integrity-building commitment to reveal who we really are – even if this leads to being disliked or rebuked – offers the best possibility of finding others equally committed to their own growth. When we are open and honest with others, a kind of natural selection occurs that leads us to those who are capable of making the kind of process commitment that can ultimately lead to a rich and enduring marriage.

Without a primary commitment to ourselves, our inner resources soon dry up and we then have very little to offer others. This accounts for the many marriages characterized by boredom, stagnation, or cynicism. The more we grow as a person, the greater our capacity to create conditions where love can flourish.

THE COMMITMENT TO ACCEPT AND UNDERSTAND ANOTHER'S WORLD

The commitment to a process of accepting and understanding another person's feelings and meanings is another significant way to express our commitment. While it is easy to believe that we care about or love a person, it is far more meaningful to put these good intentions into practice by reaching beyond ourselves to sensitively enter another's world. Expressing commitment by welcoming another's feelings and affirming his or her right to have these feelings, even if they threaten us, is one of the most effective ways to demonstrate that we love and care for a person.

Again, the capacity to really 'be there' for another rests upon an ability to validate and befriend a wide range of our own feelings. Without this fundamental commitment toward ourselves, we will lack the capacity to register the inner experiences that are a prerequisite to truly appreciating and understanding the subtle textures of another's inner world. In addition, unless we are deeply comfortable with our own feelings, it is unlikely that we will attend to another's feelings and needs with sufficient empathy.

As we come to realize some of the important meanings

concealed within our own feelings, we can more easily attune to the varied meanings inherent in another's felt experience. Having these meanings understood always feels good to people because it demonstrates our genuine concern for what is happening in their world. Other people feel supported and validated as they experience our life-affirming, non-judgmental attention – our genuine interest in who they are.

An example may clarify the intimacy-building character of accepting and understanding another's feelings. Joe, who had been involved with Kathleen for a year, began feeling angry and hurt in reaction to her unpredictable crankiness. Caring about the relationship, he wanted to know what was really happening for Kathleen. Helping her to Focus was frightening because he imagined it might lead to losing the relationship. With Joe's assistance, Kathleen began to recognize that her irritation had to do with feeling his demand that she spend more time with him. She also noticed a feeling of weakness related to not taking the time she needed to handle personal chores and relax within herself. She further experienced this as a failure of integrity – a lapse of courage to ask for what she really wanted. She then realized that the irritation had little to do with Joe, but was covering a deeper fear of losing Joe if she asked for what she wanted. She was relieved to know how she was really feeling, what it meant to her, and what she needed. As a result of processing these issues in a caring way, Joe felt closer to Kathleen. And, feeling understood, Kathleen felt a greater sense of trust and intimacy with Joe.

The effort to understand another may seem like an obvious and simple step for couples who care about each other. In reality, however, it is not. We are often preoccupied with our own fears, conflicts, and unmet needs to the exclusion of our partner's world. It is especially difficult to hear and empathize with another's experience when his or her feelings appear to threaten our own immediate needs. For instance, if she needs to be alone while he needs contact, how can each best express his or her commitment to the relationship in that moment? Or, if he is feeling hurt or angry because he desires more sexual contact, and she is hurt because sex seems more important to him than the emotional contact she needs, who will be the first to put aside personal feelings and needs in order to respond to the other?

How to resolve the complex issue of balancing our own immediate desire to be heard with another's need for understanding and support is a recurring issue in all relationships. The popular advice to compromise rarely works because it usually leads to cutting off our own feelings or to a martyr-like self-denial that creates greater resentment and conflict in the long run. A commitment to another's well-being must be balanced with a commitment to ourselves.

A great deal of self-awareness and self-affirmation is required to be a caretaker toward our own frustrations or painful feelings while the other person may be experiencing a stronger, more urgent need to be heard. In such instances, our caring, expressed as a sensitivity to another's present pain, can cue us to gently hold our own hurt or unresolved concern – that is, to just be with it internally. As our ability to be present for another is more and more integrated with a capacity to befriend and love ourselves, we may become increasingly able to temporarily place our own issues 'on hold'. Being more whole within ourselves, we may then be able to be attentive to another's feelings not out of some obligation, self-sacrifice, or desire to get something back in return, but as a spontaneous expression of concern for his or her well-being.

The commitment to honor a person's feelings and needs does not mean that we will always be able to do so on demand. Expecting this of ourselves would reflect the workings of an overly harsh inner critic. Conversely, expecting another person to always be responsive to our needs unfairly denies his or her human limitations. There will be particular times during which the burden of our own anxieties, life pressures, or unmet needs makes it difficult to accept or deal with another's feelings. If we can accept this temporary inability to extend our generosity to others, and simply be with our own feelings in a caring way, this incapacity will tend to pass.

A relationship, whether new or old, may be jeopardized if one or both parties experience a burden of unaccepted or misunderstood feelings for a continuing period of time. In such a case, it is often helpful for such an individual to communicate difficulties or discontents to the other person, or to find a third party whose assistance may lead to resolution.

THE PROCESS OF RELATING

As we come to embody a commitment to a lifestyle consistent with the values of self-affirmation, self-disclosing communication, honesty, acceptance, and understanding, then our very way of being in the world situates us in a position where trust, love, and intimacy are likely to develop with those committed to similar values. Instead of a narrowly focused search for a 'soul mate' or 'the one' who is expected to provide eternal sustenance, a process commitment calls upon us to bring a certain quality of integrity and presence into all of our relationships. As a result of doing so, meaningful friendships have an opportunity to blossom from the fertile ground created by two individuals similarly committed to their own growth.

Widening the scope of our interest to include humanity in general, our commitment becomes one of simply 'being in relationship' with those we encounter each day. 'Being in relationship' implies that we are first in contact with our own bodily felt experience and from that inner place enjoy whatever degree of contact emerges spontaneously with whomever we encounter. Consequently, an occasional 'real meeting' may take place, as the center of our being delights in the connection with the center of another's being. If we are fortunate to meet someone so deeply upon first encounter, it would be likely that this person would be able to share themselves directly and openly. Next to this, we might meet others with whom we feel a sense of excitement or satisfaction that holds the promise of potentially deeper contact. Opening to the natural process of sensitively relating to others as we stay in touch with ourselves can become a reliable basis for discerning whether we feel drawn to become better acquainted with individuals we encounter from day to day.

Following the initiation of contact, we enter a process of 'engagement.' If the initial contact was rewarding, or stimulated further interest, we may choose to become engaged in a process of becoming better acquainted with this person. In this stage we enjoy sharing *about* ourselves and doing things together. It is here that most relationships stabilize – or end – largely due to the lack of awareness and skills necessary to deepen into a potentially rich friendship.

The capacity to open to felt experience and communicate in a self-revealing manner can greatly accelerate the development of fulfilling relationships. For example, Steve found himself liking Susan after a few brief random meetings at social gatherings. He felt shy and noticed a fluttering in his stomach whenever he considered approaching her. His past pattern was to try to impress women with his sharp wit or by sharing 'sophisticated' ideas learned from one of the many growth seminars he had attended. This time, instead of trying to manipulate her into liking him, he remained with his felt experience and took the risk of telling her in a very straightforward way that he liked her and wanted to see her again. Sensing his vulnerable, genuinely felt experience, she pleasantly surprised him with the response that she also liked him and would be happy to meet again. Through this honest exchange, these two individuals had begun to achieve a level of intimacy that in the past had taken each of them many months.

When our efforts to engage another from the center of our felt experience are reciprocated with his or her authentic response, a powerful connection is created between two people. The experience of love and intimacy can intensify in rapid and unexpected ways if both people are committed to the same basic ground rule to be open to felt experience and to honestly share that experience in an unpretentious way. As trust grows through this mutuality of sharing, we feel increasingly safe to take more risks in regard to revealing who we really are – our deepest hopes, fears, hurts, and longings, as well as our vision for the future and what is truly important for us. To the degree that these further self-revelations are warmly received, understood, and reciprocated, we are inclined to feel even more intimately connected, and, perhaps, notice the stirrings of an authentic love that derives from clearly seeing one another.

A variety of blocks and fears, as well as upsets resulting from broken agreements or misunderstandings will probably arise during the process of giving birth to a friendship or marriage. It is far wiser to acknowledge and explore differences, conflicts,

or considerations as soon as we notice them than to po
dealing with them. Rather than allow such concerns to
while investing more of our time and energy into the rela
ship, we can take the responsibility to confront and work toward
resolving them in the interest of strengthening the relationship.
Or we can openly acknowledge that a deeper relationship with
this person is not wanted or not possible.

If all systems are 'go' in a budding relationship, trust can
grow to a point where we feel quite safe to be ourselves. As this
felt trust grows, so do love and intimacy, as does the process of
getting to know one another in an even more deeply felt way.
Continuing on this path, we may be gratified to discover a
person with whom we feel richly connected – a true friend.

BIRTH OF A MARRIAGE

As such friendships develop, we may realize that there is something about a particular person that enables us to touch a more
deeply felt love and joyful presence within ourselves. In addition,
we may find ourselves awakening to exciting new insights and
understandings. Through a process that is perhaps best
described by the word 'mysterious,' his or her presence somehow
helps provide a context out of which the most cherished aspects
of ourselves emerge and become increasingly embodied in our
lives.

Feeling this extraordinary sense of contact with another leads
to a greater enthusiasm about being alive, as well as feeling
more joyfully connected with life around us. 'Being in love' with
another from this fertile place within ourselves (as opposed to
'falling in love' with a person who has activated our romantic
images of an ideal mate) is closely connected with a sense of
being in love with life itself – appreciating its beauty and
preciousness, and feeling love and compassion for other living
beings with whom we share this world. In addition, we may feel
more trusting of the unpredictable, larger life process of which
we are an integral part, and more appreciatively attuned to the
surrounding environment. These and other signs may indicate
that something astonishing has taken place in relation to this
individual. A special kind of love and union has been formed

and consistently felt, partly discovered and partly created through our efforts to grow as a person.

Recognizing the birth of a union that is reliably grounded in the depths of our organismic experience, it is highly unlikely that we would lightly turn away from such a rich source of sustenance, carefully nurtured over time. Discovering that being together has steadily progressed to a degree that we *feel* married – united as one in the ground of being – we are not likely to abandon our cherished partner. We do not, however, remain together out of obligation; this stronger tie unites us. The tender place from which the marital union springs opens us to a precious bonding, a depth of connectedness that is sacred and enduring.

Experiencing a commitment derived from felt love and caring is much stronger than a formal one compelled by a sense of duty. The latter is more brittle because it is an inflexible imposition of our will or mental conviction. The former, though seemingly more fragile or tenuous, is actually more reliable because it organismically develops from the fertile ground of being. A commitment to another's growth and welfare based upon a felt sense of love and caring that derives from intimate contact with another's world of feelings and meanings is the most responsible and trustworthy commitment we can humanly make or expect another to offer.

Marriage, in its truest sense, is something that is born between two people; it is a joyful conception. On a deep level of love and intimacy, we are either married or not. And whether or not we are married in this organismic way can only be discerned in the depths of our own hearts, minds, and bodily felt experience. Deeper than, yet inclusive of, sexual attraction, it is above all else an experience of union – of being fully seen and understood. This phenomenon called 'marriage' emerges as we move toward a progressively deeper experience of love and intimacy, while maintaining a foundation of autonomy and continued personal growth.

Although we cannot exert direct control over the creation of a marriage, we do possess the ability to consent to the process whereby we grow toward the possibility of experiencing its realization. If we underestimate this ability we would be depriving ourselves of a power we possess, just as overestimating it could lead to egotistically believing that we can directly create any reality we wish (narcissistic omnipotence). We can, however, affirm the experience of connectedness we feel with another human being during the process of becoming better acquainted, and nurture conditions under which a growing trust can support a rewarding friendship or ever-deepening union. We also have the power and capacity to discern whether an initial sexual attraction or bond of 'chemistry' is sufficiently grounded in reality to form a reliable basis for a growing relationship. Slowly formed marriages are sometimes more stable ones, as intimacy grows based upon a history of shared feelings and a proven capacity to work through conflicts.

The experience of feeling connected in the way we call 'marriage' may dawn as a sudden revelation or emerge gradually as a mutually recognized reality. In either case, our excitement lies not in something we are about to do ('get married'), but in the fact that a marriage has already occurred. A formal ceremony may then celebrate this fact. A sad misunderstanding leading to much disappointment often results from the expectation that the official marriage ceremony somehow portends a new level of love or intimacy. While a short-lived honeymoon period of a few months or years may follow a formal marriage, sorrow or regret may ensue once it is discovered that the traditional ceremony, while gratifying emotion-laden romantic images of what marriage means, had no magical effect on transforming the actual felt experience of trusting or feeling more intimately connected, loved, or understood.

The transition from a socially conditioned, image-based idea of what it means to be married, to the felt experience of what love, intimacy, and marriage are really all about, may be difficult or confusing at first. But, ultimately, we can enjoy rich rewards as we trust ourselves to move toward an experientially based understanding of marriage.

THE COMMITMENT TO WORK THINGS THROUGH

Our needed sense of safety or stability in an authentic marriage derives from trusting that the other person does not want to harm us, and, in fact, wants the best for us. Since abandonment would cause intense pain, this possibility is unlikely when a gentle bond of love and empathy has firmly grown. A sense of safety is then based upon our faith in the power of our commitment to each other's well-being, which motivates us to work through any emerging conflicts or threats to the relationship.

Having experienced a marital bond of the type we are describing, we will be inclined to honor this connection, even though it may not be continuously felt. Our commitment then becomes one of honestly confronting and exploring the conflicts that periodically obscure our felt experience of love and contact. Acknowledging these obstacles as they arise provides an occasion for exploring and resolving them, learning more about ourselves, and re-discovering our love for one another.

It would be naive to imagine that once a relationship has matured to the point where we feel a marital bond that we will live in carefree bliss for the rest of our lives, untouched by the life concerns that once afflicted us. The fact remains that the world in which we live continues to impinge upon us in various ways. We still need to earn a living and interact with difficult people. We may still be carrying unresolved hurts from our past. Our self-esteem may need to grow. People with whom we feel close become ill and die. We face unpredictable experiences shared by all human beings: the prospect of pain, illness, and eventual death.

These and other stressful circumstances pose a threat and a challenge to any marriage. The threat is that one or both individuals may get off the track and become so distracted by other concerns that the experience of the subtle, tender realm of union will become obscured. Unaware of the real source of our discontent, we may make the tragic mistake of assuming that the cause of the problem somehow rests with our partner. Prematurely deciding what our discontent means, we may precipitously leave a marriage. Such an abrupt parting constitutes one of life's most painful experiences: betrayal. This betrayal reflects an invalidation or repudiation of the deeply forged bond that, for some reason, has broken down.

Even in the best of times, the experience of loving union is subject to ebb and flow. Stabilizing in a plateau-like experience of loving contact may be a gradual direction, but it would be unfair to blame ourselves or another for a periodic lessening of sexual interest or emotional connectedness. Also, the wish to spend time alone or a desire to seek the companionship of others may enrich a marriage. Occasional boredom or stagnation in relationships is sometimes a signal to broaden our base of friendships and extend our love to others. Even the best marriage cannot meet *all* of our growth needs.

Although we may be graced with the joys of a supportive marriage, our life as an individual continues – albeit with more intimacy, inspiration, and support. In an important sense, we are still alone, we must live our own lives. Unwilling to face the demands of being a distinct individual, many marriages sadly end because the so-called 'magic' suddenly seems to disappear. In reality, our inflated expectations and unrealistic dependency on the other for our sense of well-being are painfully exposed.

Another person cannot rescue us from our aloneness. Marriage does not mean enmeshment – losing ourselves in the other as we lose touch with our own personal feelings, needs, and inclinations. A distaste for acknowledging our basic aloneness in the world is a major factor contributing to conflictful or failed marriages. The capacity to be alone – a caretaker for ourselves as we grow into an autonomous individuality – provides a necessary base from which a lasting marriage can flourish.

Clearly recognizing that the very nature of a marital bond is one that is subject to blissful peaks and sullen valleys, we are better prepared to deal with these inevitable changes by maintaining a commitment to the process of working through whatever conflicts or differences arise. Recognizing and exploring these, and effectively communicating about them in the ways outlined in this book, can effectively reconnect us with a marital richness that may have been temporarily clouded.

A process approach to marriage maintains a basic trust in the depth and 'rightness' of a marriage (assuming that it evolved in the experiential manner we have described). As we face difficulties together, there emerges a faith-filled assumption, proven time and again, that our underlying connection still exists.

CHAPTER 13
Betrayal and beyond

Most married couples who break up are parting from a relationship in which a true marriage (as we have been speaking of it) never actually occurred. Although a few tender fibers of trust may have been broken, the major upset is often due to frustrated expectations regarding emotionally charged romantic images of marriage. For example, we may have hoped that marriage would permanently rescue us from feeling lonely. Due to our longing for a reliable source of love and support, we may have conveniently overlooked areas of conflict, or important ways in which we are not seeing and understanding each other.

In instances of painful separation, our upset is often calling for a re-evaluation of the ideas and hopes that are disconnected from felt experience and from the reality of how a genuine marriage is created. Without this re-evaluation, we will continue to repeat the same frustrating patterns of painful disappointment. Realizing that a mature commitment must evolve out of the growth of two autonomous individuals who are growing in themselves, we may then learn how to build the necessary foundation to support a real intimacy based upon the sharing of felt experience.

Although an individual may complain that he or she has been betrayed, a real betrayal of trust (as we are defining it) has not occurred in instances where a deeply experienced union never developed in the first place. In relationships that are primarily based on romantic beliefs and images, pain results not because there has been a breach of felt trust, but because a blind trust in these romantic hopes and expectations has failed us.

Those instances in which a relationship is growing toward a genuine marriage, or where one has already occurred, the possibility of a felt betrayal is real. In such a case, two individuals are growing together, supported by a commitment to self-honesty, open communication, and, perhaps, a deeper commitment to work things through. Then, one person suddenly balks at honestly facing unsettling personal issues, or backs off from the work necessary to resolve personal blocks or confront interpersonal difficulties.

The path to self-actualization and genuine intimacy is long, and requires a willingness to risk rejection and face hurt. This includes a readiness to be with the unresolved pain of past hurts and rejections. At times, we may be surprised to encounter such pain just as a budding relationship opens us to a place inside ourselves where we feel more deeply. As our bodies, hearts, and minds open to a more delicate, vulnerable dimension of our humanness, we may, in a flash, become suddenly aware of the wounds we are still carrying from earlier times when we were similarly vulnerable and then faced harsh rejection or a disconcerting betrayal. Dreading the prospect of re-experiencing these long forgotten hurts, we may hesitate to move toward deeper intimacy without even knowing why. Our fear may lead us to abandon others before *we* are abandoned.

Given our human vulnerabilities, it is no wonder that courage sometimes fails and we back off – retreating to familiar patterns of behavior that will eventually lead to deeper dissatisfaction. Finding ourselves opening to the delicate process of growing toward increased love and intimacy, we may feel excited to anticipate nurturing contact; and on the other hand, we may dread the possibility of a painful rejection that reminds us of past hurts. It is at this precise juncture, when our relationship is on the verge of leaping to a new level of intimacy, that the greatest possibility of betrayal arises. Just as the couple is growing closer, a fear-struck partner begins sabotaging the relationship or abandons it altogether.

Abrupt betrayal is a shocking experience. Having risked moving forward in good faith, opening the doors of self-revelation in a growing trust that we are sharing a precious journey together, we face a rude disappointment. As another door opens to unexplored or forgotten vistas within ourselves, or another communication difficulty arises, we are suddenly left standing alone. The person with whom we were growing in trust and love has disappeared. Instead, we face a blaming, hostile 'demon' who suddenly sees nothing good in the relationship and now wants nothing to do with us. In this situation, the unwillingness to face and communicate our actual feelings constitutes a betrayal of the commitment to self-honesty, openness to the other, and (if the commitment has so progressed) working things through.

Another face of betrayal appears when one person abandons the commitment to his or her own growth while remaining in the relationship. Unwilling to honestly face felt experience within oneself, personal growth stagnates. Withholding the very essence of what it means to be human – a vulnerable core that includes tears and joy – the relationship is robbed of the richness that it is capable of. As a result, the very source of the marital union or potential union dries up. This quiet withdrawal of contact inevitably alienates the other person, although he or she may only be in touch with a vague sense of sadness, bewilderment, or self-blame.

In the above case we may not experience the acute hurt of abrupt betrayal, yet we are faced with a frustrating and chronically painful emotional betrayal. Observing this, we may be moved to confront the person with our honest feelings and unmet needs. If our efforts at dialogue consistently lead to unsatisfying outcomes (if the other person refuses to grow or fails to recognize the ways in which he or she needs to grow), we may then need to take care of ourselves by separating from the relationship.

Betrayal is one of the most complex and traumatic life experiences that you may encounter on the path toward self-actualization and true intimacy. We briefly discuss it here in order to offer support and encouragement if you are facing such a crisis (or continue to be affected by past wounds). It is at a time like this that you are most likely to abandon your own journey, giving up hope that true love can really be found, or that you have any power to change the unhappy course of events. Reacting to the burden of your grief, you may make the quiet choice to close down a vital center of aliveness inside yourself.

The experience of betrayal calls upon us to draw from inner resources in order to remain with our felt experience and learn from it what we may in order to move forward in our lives. A period of grieving, subsequent to terminating contact, is often necessary. To forgo grieving is to neglect our organism's natural way of healing itself by releasing pain and re-orienting us in a direction that would better meet our needs. Grieving allows our organism to remain open. Discouraged by betrayal, we may choke off emotions and harden into a cynical, pessimistic, or embittered stance toward life. This hardening against our feelings actually intensifies the pain of betrayal.

Betrayal calls upon us to be a caretaker for our hurt. Supportive friends can also be invaluable during such a time. In fact, deep friendships have a unique opportunity to blossom (once we risk sharing our sorrow with others). During such a time, we are more sensitively aware of who is really present to us and who is not emotionally available. Although a good friend may not substitute for the richness of a marriage or a hoped-for union, opening to new sources of nurturing can remind us of what is important in life and empower us to continue our journey.

Ultimately we travel alone in life, although we are greatly enriched by being with those who can truly see us and with whom we can freely give and receive love. A time of betrayal challenges us to maintain an openness to life and a basic trust in ourselves and the life process. Courageously re-affirming ourselves and the commitment to our own growth, we can find the wisdom necessary to achieve personal fulfillment, connectedness with others, and a harmonious relationship with the larger life process in which we participate.

CHAPTER 14
Conclusion: implications for a world at peace

Many of us live with the silent fear that our needs for acceptance, intimacy, and love may never be satisfied. This fear may be based upon our experience growing up if, in fact, such needs were not adequately met. If we have a history of being criticized and manipulated, rather than trusted, we may be handicapped in relation to developing trusting, intimate relationships. Unfulfilled in our basic needs, we may come to view others suspiciously or as adversaries in a competitive struggle to survive.

Abraham Maslow's research into the factors that lead to healthy growth and self-actualization, plus the findings of numerous other informed observers, suggests a common trend. Once satisfied in the basic needs for food, shelter, safety, and belonging, individuals are naturally inclined to move toward actualizing their greater potential for happiness and well-being. This direction involves a recognition of our need for connectedness and harmonious relations with the other beings with whom we share this planet. Since, as we grow, deeper fulfillment resides in enjoying our contact with one another, it follows that the only reliable pathway toward this goal is learning how to be caring toward the feelings and needs of others.

It is difficult, however, to meet others' needs if we ourselves remain chronically unfulfilled. And so we are faced with the reality of a deprived humanity struggling to pick themselves up by their own bootstraps, while being called upon to be sensitive to other people. However, there is a hopeful note. Never before has there been so much psychological knowledge regarding how to recognize and meet our genuine needs. Tools such as Focusing can help us be in touch with ourselves in a way that gradually leads to removing obstacles to our growth. As we touch ourselves more deeply, we develop inner resources that enable us to be more attuned and responsive to others' needs.

As more and more individuals grow in this way, society as a whole will begin to transform in positive ways. Chronic social problems such as crime, alcoholism, and child abuse are generated by years of growing up in an environment that has failed to support individuals in meeting their needs for acceptance, self-esteem, and intimacy. As we clearly recognize the cause of social ills that affect all of us, we will realize the paramount importance of effectively introducing personal awareness skills and communication skills into our public school systems and other institutions.

Interestingly, not only is interpersonal fulfillment and social order dependent upon the fulfillment of fundamental needs, but even the keys to gradual disarmament and world peace lie in assisting others to meet the basic necessities of physical sustenance, belonging, and self-esteem. The lessons of history are far too sobering to deny the global advantages of nurturing these perennial needs of humanity. People who are hungry, unrecognized, or excluded tend to be fearful and hostile. And those who are ridiculed or humiliated often become violent in response to a threat to their self-worth.

Never before have we been so close to the possibility of mass destruction. Governments now possess the means to destroy planetary life in an instant. Resolving the international tensions that could lead to disaster must begin with the sober choice to grow more in touch with ourselves. Through discovering our own actual needs, fears, and hopes, we touch a tender chord that unites us in our humanness with others. It is only through learning to be in touch with our felt experience that we will discover a road to peace both within ourselves and with each other.

That which exists within ourselves can be observed to exist between each other and between nations – as within, so without. The key to an eventual global disarmament is a decision within each of us to 'disarm' ourselves. As we begin to notice and relinquish our own defensive response with each other, we invite mutual disarmament.

As we gently open to our felt experience and become willing

to share our experience, we spontaneously invite others to do the same. As we discover our own feelings, we develop a facility to sense the same feelings in our fellow human beings. As we learn to experience a deeply felt caring for ourselves, we tend to develop a corresponding caring for the well-being of those whose lives we touch. As this mutually reinforcing process spreads among people, so may it gradually spread globally – leading to the reduction of arms and increase in mutual understanding that is now necessary for our very survival.

This process of learning to contact and communicate our authentic felt experience requires time, but so do all lasting changes. Perhaps it can occur more rapidly in our present age due to advances in the psychology of personal growth and non-violent communication. Any one of us could make a small, yet significant contribution by developing the awareness and skills that lead to the growth of trust and intimacy.

Appendixes

APPENDIX A
The Focusing steps

PREPARATION:

Take some time to become quiet. . . (pause). Allow your attention to settle inside your body. Just be with how you feel. . . (pause at least one minute).

1 CLEARING A SPACE BY TAKING AN INVENTORY

(a) Allowing your attention to remain inside your body, notice if there's anything going on in your life that's getting in the way of feeling really good right now . . . (pause: wait for response).

(b) Can you put that aside for now?. . . (Wait until there is a sense of putting it aside. If, after several attempts, you cannot set it aside, proceed to step 2.)

(c) Is there anything else going on in your life that's getting between you and feeling good right now?. . .

(d) Just notice that whole thing and see if you can set it aside for now.

(e) If those were all resolved, would there by anything else getting in the way of feeling really good?

(f) Can you put that aside?

(g) Anything else?

(Continue in this manner, repeating steps (f) and (g) until your inventory feels complete. You might ask yourself, 'Would I feel really good right now if all of these issues were resolved?'

(h) Is there anything else in your life that is not a problem, but that would like attention now? (If so, set it aside as well.)

2 SENSING WHICH ONE WANTS ATTENTION RIGHT NOW

(a)   Of all these issues that came up for you, which one feels the heaviest, stands out the most, or is calling for attention right now?. . .

3 IS IT OKAY TO BE WITH THIS?

(a)   Is it okay to be with this for awhile? Just check to see if your body says 'yes' or 'no' (pause. . . If 'yes,' go to step 3.) (If it's not okay, ask):

(b)   Is it okay to be with how scary or difficult it is to get in touch with this right now? (If 'yes,' notice how your body feels about this. Then, when you feel ready, proceed to step 3; if the answer is still 'no,' then notice if there's another issue that feels okay to be with.)

4 ALLOWING A FELT SENSE TO FORM

(a)   How does this whole thing feel inside your body right now?. . . (pause)

(b)   Where in your body do you feel it?. . .

(c)   What does it feel like?. . .

(d)   Take some time to sense it inside of yourself, apart from your thoughts about it. . .

5 ALLOWING IT TO EXPRESS ITSELF

(a)   As you stay with how your body is experiencing the whole thing, allow a word, phrase, or image to come that expresses how you feel inside. . .

(b)   Just allow yourself to be with that whole sense of ——— (whatever word, phrase, image, etc. came up). If anything more wants to come to you as you stay with that (whether a new word, phrase, image, memory, or felt meaning), then allow it to come. (Continue in this manner, using step (b) to open to each new experience as it arises. If something particularly painful or difficult emerges, see if you can be with it in a gentle, caring way.)

(After several cycles, when you sense that there has been some release, you may ask):

(c) Does that feel complete for now, or is there something that would like more attention? (If complete, go to step 6. If not, return to step (b); or, if you are feeling stuck, proceed to ask one of the following optional questions):

(d) Optional step: asking

    1   Exploratory questions:

      — Staying with how your body is experiencing the whole issue or situation, notice if you get any sense of what that's about.

      — What's the main thing about all this that's really getting to you?

      — What's the worst thing about it?

      — What is it about this whole issue you're dealing with that has you feeling so ———? (whatever word or phrase that may have arisen that matches your felt sense).

    2   Forward-moving questions (remember to allow your attention to be inside your body as you work with any of these questions):

      — Do you have a sense of what direction would feel like a small step forward with all this?

      — What direction would feel like a breath of fresh air?

      — What needs to happen in order to feel better about the whole situation?. . . Is anything getting in the way of that happening?

6 ALLOWING YOURSELF TO BE

Just allow yourself to be with how you feel inside right now, perhaps with a sense of appreciation for whatever steps you may have taken.

APPENDIX B
Troubleshooting reference guide

You will probably encounter various obstacles and difficulties while Focusing, particularly when first learning the process. While there is no substitute for a skilled facilitator who can artfully address your specific difficulties and unique needs, you may consult this guide when you feel stuck, confused, or unsure of your next step in Focusing. These suggestions may also be useful for guiding another person through the process of Focusing.

(A) *Are you having difficulty getting in touch with feelings or a felt sense in relation to the issue at hand?*

POSSIBLE REASONS:
(1)   Most of your attention is in your head, rather than in your body.
(2)   Your inner critic is quietly at work, diverting attention from the more subtle undercurrents of your felt experience.
(3)   There is a 'loud' background feeling that you are unaware of.
(4)   You are trying too hard.

POSSIBLE SOLUTIONS:
(1)   If you notice yourself thinking about the issue, or trying to figure out a solution, see if you can gently return your attention to how your body is feeling, perhaps by bringing awareness to the area of your stomach and chest. You may do this each time you notice yourself wandering into thoughts disconnected from your felt experience.
     You could also try taking a few slow, deep breaths. On the

exhalation, let your attention flow deep down into your body. Let your eyes be closed or gently cast down a few feet in front of you. Then, with your attention resting inside your body, say, 'I feel really good about this whole thing (whatever issue you are working with), don't I?' Then, notice what comes that says 'not really.' That will be a felt sense that can then be Focused on.

(2) If you are being plagued by a critical voice – one that tells you what you should or shouldn't be feeling, or that you are bad, wrong, selfish, etc. – just notice that your inner critic has arisen. Or, you may notice a cynical, doubting voice telling you that you will remain stuck and unhappy in your life, or that you will not get anywhere with Focusing. This may be experienced as a haunting, tiresome background feeling that keeps you psychologically imprisoned.

You can tell this inner critic or inner cynic to 'get off your back.' You may need to do this rather assertively in order to make it known that you mean business. If you happen to become aware of people who have criticized you during your life (such as a parent, teacher, or friend), you may want (in your mind's eye) to tell these people to leave you alone.

As another option, you can notice whatever feelings arise that are associated with the appearance of the inner critic. Then allow yourself to be with these feelings in a gentle, caring way.

You may also dialogue with your critic, asking what it wants in order to let you be. Or, refer to the previous chapter on the inner critic for further assistance.

If your inner critic frequently returns to interfere with Focusing, you may benefit by getting appropriate professional assistance to resolve this particularly obstinate hindrance to Focusing.

(3) Sometimes there is a vague, background feeling that obscures awareness of all other experience. Like gravity, it profoundly affects us although we may be unaware of its influence. By paying close attention, we may begin to identify it and experience its impact. Perhaps, for instance, there is a sense of being driven, or a prevailing feeling of sadness, annoyance, guilt, worry, or helplessness in your life. You may then direct your Focusing toward the main feeling, perhaps entering a new doorway to unexplored regions of yourself.

(4) If you notice yourself trying too hard or wondering whether you are Focusing properly or just remaining in your head, try to set those considerations aside for now. Take a deep breath, and gently return to your bodily felt sense of the issue at hand. Relax and patiently wait as you carefully attend to your felt experience. Focusing takes time! Don't push yourself! But if you do, just notice the pushing and allow your awareness to return to your body by becoming gently aware of your breathing.

(B) *Are you losing the felt sense before experiencing any distinct release of shift?*

POSSIBLE REASONS:
(1) You returned to your usual thinking mode or your inner critic is active again.
(2) You have lost a sense of connectedness between your bodily felt sense and the relevant issue.
(3) You have become lost in an image.

POSSIBLE SOLUTIONS:
(1) Being self-critical or overly identified with your usual thoughts may be dealt with by using any of the previous suggestions.
(2) If you lose the sense of connection between your issue and the related bodily felt sense, first see if the felt sense of that issue wants to return. Then stay with the whole sense of whatever issue is there. If it does not return, check whether that issue is still there for you, perhaps by saying, 'This feels fine now, doesn't it?' If something comes, resume Focusing on your felt sense of this concern. If a new issue emerges during this process that *feels* more charged or relevant, you may switch your attentions to this new concern.
(3) Sometimes images have a life of their own. If you find yourself 'floating off' with an image, or notice that one image quickly changes into another, take some time to return to your body sense of one particular image. Notice how this image *feels* inside you, as opposed to analyzing it or being mesmerized by it. Being grounded in your body provides a base from which change and resolution can occur.

(C) *Do you feel dreamy or 'spaced out?'*

POSSIBLE REASONS:
(1)   You have entered a meditative state.
(2)   You have entered an unfamiliar or mildly altered state of consciousness.
(3)   You are getting sleepy. You may be chronically fatigued. Or you may be tired from a busy day or lack of adequate sleep.

POSSIBLE SOLUTIONS:
(1)   Meditators who try Focusing sometimes enter a familiar experience they usually arrive at through their particular form of meditation. Remember: Focusing involves quietly sitting with a felt sense of a particular issue, and then noticing whatever naturally arises out of your bodily felt sense as a result of being with this issue. Focusing is different than just being with your breathing or noticing physiological states separate from life concerns. Also, you may be more aware of your bodily felt sense when keeping your eyes open or gently cast down.
(2)   You may have entered a diffuse or pleasantly altered state of consciousness. Again, remember to return your attention to your body and to an awareness of the original issue. Or, starting fresh, notice whatever wants attention now.
(3)   If you get tired or sleepy, try opening your eyes and taking a deep breath. If this is not enough, you might try opening a window to get fresh air or walking around the room. If you frequently get tired while Focusing, you may want to Focus on that phenomenon itself, asking 'How does it feel to always be tired when I try to Focus?' Perhaps some new understanding or fresh perspective will emerge if there are emotional aspects to the problem.
   The tiredness may also be caused by poor nutrition or inadequate exercise. Positive changes in these areas, accompanied by whatever nutritional or medical assistance may be necessary, may help correct the imbalance. Or it may just be that you simply need to get some sleep; if so, try Focusing at a later time.

(D) *Do you seem to be Focusing, but no resolution comes?*

POSSIBLE REASONS:
(1) You may not be allowing adequate time for the process to naturally lead to a felt shift.
(2) You have not yet found a skillfully-worded question that could help the process unfold.
(3) You are unrealistically expecting a mental or practical solution to a bodily felt problem.
(4) You are expecting too big a shift.

POSSIBLE SOLUTIONS:
(1) Waiting is a skill that is repeatedly necessary for effective Focusing. Be willing not to know the answer, or, if that is uncomfortable, Focus on what it feels like to have no answer. Is it OK to just 'hang out' with a feeling and allow it to take its natural course? Can you tolerate an ambivalent, vague, or uncomfortable situation until your bodily felt wisdom is ready to speak? If not, what gets in the way? You can then Focus on whatever comes in response to this. As you learn through your own experience that waiting often leads to surprising, and, at times, astonishing results, you may become increasingly willing to sit with a cold, hard, dark place within yourself, until it reveals something of itself.

Another approach is to use Gendlin's step of imagining your-self putting your arm around the issue, or holding it on your lap. Developing a friendly, caring relationship with a difficult concern can often soften it so that some movement may be enjoyed.
(2) Try asking an appropriate forward-moving question (see step 4 of the Focusing Guide) that seems well matched to the situation. Work with your Focusing facilitator (if you have one) to formulate just the right question to help your inner process unfold. If you get a word that matches the quality of your bodily felt sense, you may try to ask a question that connects this with the original issue. For example, you can ask, 'What is it about this relationship that feels so heavy?' (or jumpy, sticky, hard, pressured, or whatever word has come).
(3) Expecting a solution from your head, or a practical answer to a painful issue misses the point of Focusing. The goal is not to find a solution, although one may spontaneously occur. The main goal in Focusing is to learn how to enter the process of

being with your felt experience. That, in itself, feels satisfying because you are then allowing yourself to have contact with a deeper aspect of who you are. Directly attending to your felt experience in a friendly, allowing way opens a pathway toward feeling internally free of the problem. That's what you really want. A solution from your mind is not nearly as satisfying as a resolution experienced through touching the depth of your bodily felt experience. Feeling internally relieved may then lead to a practical step forward, such as expressing anger or sadness to a friend. But the action in itself will be empty unless it is associated with a genuinely felt experience of resolution.

(4) If you set your goals too high, you may create disappointment for yourself. You may also be overlooking the small, yet significant, shifts that are already happening inside you. Appreciate whatever subtle releases or openings are happening, and take some time to notice how you feel after each small shift.

APPENDIX C
Tips for the Focusing guide

Here are some suggestions for guiding a person through the Focusing steps. Throughout this section, the word 'Focuser' is used to refer to the person who is being led through Focusing. The word 'guide' refers to the person who is facilitating.

1 Allow the Focuser to be in charge

As helpers, we tend to want to be in control in order to do a good job or prove our competence. In Focusing, the Focuser is the one in charge. Let him or her be responsible for whatever comes up. It is the Focuser who chooses what to explore or whether to Focus on any particular issues and each successive felt sense as it arises. You are there to support and facilitate the process. Your gentle, caring presence can have a surprisingly potent effect on facilitating the unfolding of the Focuser's felt experience.

We recommend that you read the questions directly from the Focusing guide, at least until you become familiar with the steps. Your role in asking these questions and being sensitively present can help direct the Focuser to his or her felt experience. Do not push, challenge, or interrogate the Focuser. Just allow time for his or her inner process to gradually unfold.

2 Do not interpret or give advice

Offering advice, analyzing, or interpreting what *you* think is happening is most often not helpful to the Focuser. Just stay with Focusing, without mixing in any of *your* ideas. Even if they are accurate, they are rarely useful, and may even interfere. Do not add insight to injury! Answers discovered within oneself are more poignant and transformative than those originating from an outside source. Your empathic presence is your strongest asset for providing a safe climate to help the Focuser stay attuned to his or her bodily felt wisdom regarding important life issues.

After concluding a session, you may share some of your own perceptions and related experiences if they seem helpful. If you do so, it is often best to be brief. Remember that the Focuser may appreciate some quiet time to digest the effects of the Focusing session.

3 Ask the questions in a deliberate, slowly-paced manner

Pacing is a key aspect of guiding. This skill can become more refined with practice. Also, since people proceed at varying paces, you can learn by asking for feedback after a session. The Focuser is your best source of information regarding whether you spoke too quickly or slowly, or asked too many or too few questions. The Focuser can also give you feedback regarding whether your voice quality was warm and inviting, or harsh and mechanical. You may also inquire about what he or she found to be helpful and what was experienced as intrusive or unhelpful. Asking for honest feedback in the spirit of learning can be the quickest way to fine tune your skills as a guide.

Generally speaking, proceed at a slow, deliberate pace. Remember that it takes time for subtle, felt experience to reveal itself. Allow at least two or three minutes of silence before becoming concerned whether the Focuser is stuck or perplexed. Sometimes a silent period of up to five or even ten minutes is necessary in order for a bodily felt sense to form or in order for a vague felt sense to become more crystallized.

4 Proceed gently when something potentially painful arises

Anytime you sense that an issue or feeling has come that is particularly painful, scary, or difficult, ask 'Is it okay to be with this?' This question introduces a sense of safety into the Focusing process. If something is not okay to be with, ask if he or she can take a step back and be with the fear itself or put a friendly arm around the discomforting feeling. Unable to do so, he or she may want to work with a different concern, or a smaller aspect of a large, overwhelming issue. Or, they may want to stop Focusing altogether. If they would like to stop, do not take it personally. Some individuals need professional help with complex or painful issues that have gone unheeded for a long time.

5 Become familiar with the terrain of your own felt experience

Knowing yourself provides the most reliable foundation for effectively guiding others. If you are uncomfortable with certain feelings inside yourself, this discomfort has a way of being conveyed to others, which can have a dampening effect on their process. Through nonverbal communication or an unskillful verbal intervention, your uneasiness with feelings such as anger, sadness, fear, or even joy may be picked up. This may lead them to feel unsafe to further experience or express vulnerable feelings. As you become increasingly friendly with all aspects of your own felt experience, you will convey a sense of acceptance and non-judgmental openness to a wide range of experience. This creates a trusting atmosphere for others to risk sharing their honest experience. As you become more comfortable with your own hopes, hurts, and fears, your capacity to provide an empathic environment for others will increase.

YOUR OPTIONS AS A FOCUSING FACILITATOR

1 Just listening

Just listening with care and understanding, with an eye toward understanding the Focuser's feelings and meanings, can have a healing effect. The simple capacity to listen, without the compulsion to state your opinions or rescue a person from his or her pain, can help support the natural unfolding of a person's bodily felt experience and inner wisdom. By being in contact with the center of your own bodily felt experience, you can learn to listen from a deep, quiet place that reflects caring, compassion, and love.

2 Repeating

You can repeat back the exact word or phrase of the Focuser. Echoing his or her precise wording can sometimes sharpen a felt sense or provide a new vista. In addition, becoming aware of the felt quality of his or her words can provide a sense of how the person is experiencing what he or she is saying. This can lead to more supportive contact between the Focuser and yourself. If the Focuser has expressed several feelings or meanings, you might repeat back one or two of these that seem particularly charged or poignant to you.

3 Reflecting

This response reflects back the crux of the meaning that you have heard. You may combine the Focuser's words with some of your own, or express solely in your own words your understanding of what has been said. This can be especially helpful if the Focuser is repeatedly struggling to find the right words to express an experience. You may then offer something that you sense may fit. But, be sure to quickly forgo your own choice of words if he or she does not respond to them – otherwise you may divert attention from his or her own felt process. Reflecting back the central meaning that you are hearing may also be helpful when you feel overwhelmed by many words. This enables the Focuser to hear back a condensed version of what he or she is saying. However, if the Focuser indicates that you have missed the point, listen to this feedback and return to your primary task of helping to guide his or her attention back to bodily felt experience.

4 Checking

'Checking' may be used in order to help the Focuser check whether an emerging word, phrase, or meaning 'feels' right ('right' in the sense of accurate). This allows the Focuser to sense the 'fit' of what has been said with the bodily felt sense. The guide may ask, 'Does that say it? If not, notice what comes that might express it better.' The appropriate use of this intervention can also help the Focuser deepen into an experience that feels on target. Checking can be especially helpful when:

(a) You sense that they may be speaking more from their thoughts than from their bodily felt sense.
(b) They are having difficulty remaining with a felt sense.
(c) You want to give them time to deepen into their felt sense.

5 Leading

You are leading when you ask skillful questions intended to facilitate the unfolding of the Focuser's felt experience. This involves use of the Focusing steps or slight variations of them once you become familiar with the basic instructions. The sensitive asking of exploratory or forward-moving questions has a way of touching and gradually bringing forth an individual's deeply felt wisdom.

6 Giving up

If you ever feel lost or confused as a guide, that's okay. Just acknowledge this, and work together with the Focuser to sense a direction that may move the process forward. You, as a guide, do not have the responsibility to make a session go well. A cooperative effort to formulate a useful question or sense what is now wanting attention might provide a novel opening that helps the Focuser re-connect with the richness of his or her inner world.

OTHER HELPFUL INTERVENTIONS

1 Are you being flooded with words or explanations?

You might ask, 'What feels like the main thing for you right now?' Or, 'What's the main thing that wants attention in all of that?' This can help focus attention.

2 Is there a long pause of several minutes or more?

If you sense that the Focuser may be lost or is moving away from his or her felt sense, you may say something such as, 'When you feel like it, let me know what's happening for you.' This allows the Focuser to stay inside his or her process if something meaningful is happening, while reminding him or her of your continued interest and desire to be helpful. Extended periods of quiet are often very productive, so be patient. If you are feeling impatient with the Focuser's pace, notice if it relates to your own discomfort with silence.

3 Do they seem to be intellectualizing (in their heads)?

Signs that the Focuser may be intellectualizing include lengthy explanations, rapid talking, or your own felt sense of confusion or being overwhelmed. You may then ask a question that helps ground the Focuser, such as 'Are you experiencing what you're saying right now?' or, 'Do you have a bodily sense of that?' However, such questions may be distracting or annoying if the Focuser really is with his or her felt experience. Therefore, limit such inquiries to those times when you are fairly confident that the Focuser has moved away from his or her feelings.

4 Is the Focuser stuck?

You might ask him or her to put aside Focusing for now and spend some time just talking about the issue. Some relevant aspect may then appear that has a 'feltness' to it. You may then assist him or her to begin Focusing on this emerging feeling.

APPENDIX D
A guide to initiating relationships

In order to create a satisfying intimate relationship, we must acknowledge our need for contact and be willing to reach out for what we want. Caring for ourselves by accepting this need allows us to live more and more from a place inside ourselves where a genuine 'meeting' with others is possible.

As we learn to live from our bodily felt sense, we begin to discern more clearly whether those we encounter are similarly 'home' in themselves. If so, we will tend to feel more alive in their presence. Enjoying even a moment of genuine contact, we may be moved to want additional time together to explore what there may be between us. This calls upon us to express our desire for his or her companionship, which requires a willingness to risk being hurt if we are rejected. Through an ability to be a caretaker for our hurt or embarrassment, we will gain the confidence necessary to honestly reach out to people whom we like.

It is usually necessary to experience a number of close relationships at some point in our lives in order to distinguish between what we really want from what we think we want. These 'learning relationships' as psychologist Susan Campbell (1983) calls them, help us become clearer about what we minimally need to be fulfilled in a committed relationship. These 'basic minimum requirements' (BMRs) are unique to each of us. Since saying 'yes' to a growing commitment in one relationship implies saying 'no' to other ones, it is important to be as clear as possible regarding the 'rightness' of an involvement.

Some individuals may have few BMRs. For them, the experience of love and intimacy may be sufficient. For others, these may not be enough to sustain a lifelong commitment. Besides a fundamental love and affinity, there may be other needs when choosing a partner. These may include factors such as our personal interests, as well as our age and place in life. For example, if we clearly want to have children, then a basic requirement is to be with someone who also has this particular interest. Becoming deeply involved with a person who does not want children could be very unsettling at some point later in the relationship. This inevitable pain could be averted by acknowledging and acting upon our felt need as soon as we become aware of it.

BMRs may also include factors such as an acceptable age range and geographic distance, or a requirement that the person has no other primary involvement and is ready for a committed relationship. If you are at a life stage where you want a serious relationship while the other person is in an exploring stage, it may be wise not to become more deeply involved. You might also want to be with someone who is engaged in a similiar profession as your own, or, perhaps, a person committed to a career that he or she feels good about. Feelings about monogamy may also be important to discuss at an early point if there are strong feelings about this.

Even if you are not fully in agreement on all accounts, you may feel confident to move forward in the relationship if you sense an openness to discuss concerns that each of you can be flexible with. But if you feel resolute about something for which the other person has an equally strong opposing need, you may choose to take care of yourself by giving up the goal of partnership and moving toward a friendship.

Honoring our BMRs when they are truly based upon experience (rather than romantic images or inflated expectations) can be a skillful way to fulfill two primary needs in life: our growth as autonomous individuals and our need for love and intimacy.

Here are some preliminary questions to help you explore issues and feelings regarding the initiation of a relationship. Take a minute or so to allow your attention to restfully settle inside your body before reading these questions. Then notice what comes in response. You may work with the question(s) that feels most relevant to you. Or, begin with question 1; if nothing comes, then proceed to question 2, etc.

If something comes as you work with any of these questions,

take some time to sense what you are experiencing inside yourself. If you wish to explore this further, proceed to step 3 of the
Focusing steps.

(1) Is there anything missing in your life right now that could
    be satisfied through an intimate relationship?. . .
(2) How do you feel about the possibility of having an intimate
    relationship?. . .
(3) Can you get a sense of how you would feel to have a
    fulfilling relationship?. . . (take some time to feel this inside
    yourself). Now, does anything get in the way of that
    happening?. . .
(4) Is there anything going on inside of you that's getting in
    the way of having a close relationship?. . .
(5) Does anything need to change inside yourself before you
    would feel open to an intimate relationship?. . .
(6) Do you notice any past hurts that you're still carrying
    inside that are getting in the way of being more open to
    people?. . .
(7) Do you have a sense of what you want in a close
    relationship?. . .
(8) Does anything get in the way of approaching a person you
    like?. . .

APPENDIX E
A guide to improving relationships

Once you become familiar with Focusing, you may use this guide to clarify and resolve important relationship issues. You may use it by yourself or be assisted by another person. You might also experiment with being guided by the very person who is the object of your Focusing. However, some preliminary degree of trust is necessary in order to feel safe to allow an unfolding of your inner process in the company of your partner. Focusing together can be a very intimate process. Therefore, you may not want to do so unless you feel reasonably safe, or have faith that trust and intimacy could grow through being vulnerable with each other in this way. As one client put it:

> 'I don't want to bare my soul when I'm in a place of not trusting her. Focusing with her on a concern about the relationship already shows there's trust. It's like saying, "I trust you enough to do a Focusing session and bare my guts to you." '

In relationships where trust is tentative or has faltered, a skilled therapist or Focusing guide is often helpful. Instances of critical, intrusive communications can then be gently pointed out, and each person can be coached to express honest feelings and needs free from the threat of hurtful judgments and unproductive accusations.

This guide may also be used as a preventive measure. Interpersonal issues that you may not be fully aware of, or ones that seem insignificant, are more likely to be resolved when addressed before they have a chance to fester.

Be aware that if you are experiencing some other pressing life concern, it may be difficult to Focus on the relationship. For instance, if you have just lost your job or are troubled with a health concern, you may first need to explore these issues using the basic Focusing steps.

Preparation:

Take some time to become quiet . . . (pause). Allow your attention to settle inside your body. Just be with how you feel . . . (pause at least one minute).

1 Taking an inventory

(a)   Allowing your attention to remain inside your body, notice if there's anything getting in the way of feeling really good about the relationship right now. (If something comes, just be aware of it without exploring it right now.)

(b)   Can you put that whole concern aside for now? (Wait until there is a sense of setting it aside. If, after several attempts, it cannot be set aside, then proceed to step 2 of the Focusing steps.)

(c)   If this concern were all resolved, would there be anything else missing in this relationship?

(d)   Can you put that aside for now?

(e)   Is there anything else getting in the way of enjoying this relationship?

(f)   Can you set that aside for now?

(Continue in this manner, repeating steps (e) and (f) until your inventory feels complete. You may ask yourself, 'Would I feel really good about the relationship if all of these issues were resolved?'. . .)

(g)   Of all these concerns that came up for you, which one feels the heaviest, stands out the most, or is calling for attention right now?. . .

Now proceed to step 3 of the Focusing steps on page 168. If you feel stuck at some point, you may turn to the following questions: Remember to allow your attention to rest inside your body as you respond to these questions.

– What's the most dissatisfying thing about the relationship?
What's the main thing you're missing?
– What direction would help you feel more at peace in this
relationship?
– What direction would help you feel a greater sense of integrity?
– Do you need something in order to feel more satisfied in the
relationship?
– Is there something you need to give to yourself in order to
feel better about the relationship? Does something need to
change inside of you?

If something arises, take some time to be with how that feels
inside you; then return to step 4a of the Focusing steps.

APPENDIX F

Additional suggestions for couples or friends who want to Focus together

The following suggestions are for the person in a relationship who is acting as the Focusing guide. The person who is being led is called the Focuser.

1 Have a clear understanding that this is the Focuser's time

When your partner or friend is processing a delicate issue, there is often the temptation to give advice, console, or challenge his or her perspective. This tendency is particularly strong when he or she is exploring an issue that directly relates to you. Remember that whatever thoughts, feelings, and concerns your partner or friend may be having have an opportunity to be resolved once they are out in the open. If you have the impulse to dispute a fact, challenge an assumption, or even offer reassurance, your role as guide is generally best served by just noticing these reactions without expressing them. This can be an opportunity for you to be a caretaker for whatever feelings and reactions are occurring inside you; just be with them in a quiet, caring way. Acting them out can interfere with the natural unraveling of the Focuser's inwardly felt process. Once the session is complete, then you will have an opportunity to express yourself.

Occasionally the Focuser might find it helpful to ask for clarification regarding some point. Or, he or she may want to inquire about your motivation or intention related to some incident. You may then share your own view of the facts as you see them, or reveal what is happening in your inner world in regard to his or her concern. This may help clarify something for the Focuser. Remember, however, to return to your role as guide as soon as possible in order to maintain the continuity and momentum of the process.

The surest antidote for the impulse to interrupt our friend's or partner's Focusing session is to participate in at least one session in which he or she experiences a felt shift. As you learn through your own experience that resolutions do happen, it becomes easier to tolerate just being there while your friend methodically Focuses on critical issues and feelings that may have some impact on you. Knowing that change is likely to come by faithfully staying with the process gives you confidence to 'hang in there' while you or your partner may be in a painful or difficult place.

Directly experiencing positive changes through helping your friend or partner be with his or her felt experience can provide inspiration to be more honest and open with each other. Instead of talking in our customary ways and soon getting stuck (thus regretting that we talked about it at all), we will then have discovered for ourselves a new pattern than can lead to more intimacy and fulfillment.

2 Interrupt the Focuser if you feel overwhelmed

If the Focuser is exploring a concern that begins to overwhelm you to the degree that you are no longer able to listen effectively, then you may tell him or her what is happening for you. If you are overwhelmed with feelings such as fear, sorrow, or frustration, you may need to attend to these emerging feelings that have been stirred up in you. The Focuser may then agree to switch roles temporarily, provided that it is not too disruptive to do so. If it is too discomforting, you may both need to Focus on your own for awhile.

Before interrupting a session, try to be with your reactive feelings within yourself. If they are rather strong, you may tell the Focuser that you need a minute or so just to be with yourself. Stating this will act as a signal for him or her to continue Focusing quietly without your assistance, until you give some sign that your full attention has returned.

3 Work out an interactional system that is effective for both of you

Through experimenting, you may discover a format that works for each of your needs. Once you learn how to Focus, you can work out signals (such as raising your hand, nodding your head, or simply stating what you want) to indicate that you now want to be quietly with yourself or that you would like some guidance or dialogue.

You can also work out an agreement regarding whether it is okay to interrupt the Focuser to offer simple clarifications that can be stated with a minimum of words. For instance, as the guide, you have a missing piece of information that you think would help the Focuser; you may say something such as, 'Can I say something here that might be helpful?' or 'Can I clarify something here?' For instance, if the Focuser is upset that you were late for an appointment, you might say, 'I understood that we were to meet at 6 o'clock, not 5 o'clock.' Then the Focuser may realize that it was not your intention to be late. However, interrupting in this manner has its pitfalls. Blurting out a clarification may be experienced as disruptive, however helpful you may imagine it to be. Also, what you may consider to be a simple fact may actually be your interpretation of an event. For instance, if the Focuser feels hurt because you were late for dinner, you may want to interrupt to clarify your intentions. However, this may lead to an unproductive argument. If such interruptions frequently lead to conflict, it is often best to see if you can put your own concerns aside until the other person is ready to hear from you. Even if there is a misperception or lack of information, a surprising resolution may occur by simply Focusing on felt experience.

Another matter you can explore through your own experience is whether it is helpful to Focus alone before doing so with your friend or partner. Doing so may enable you to sort out issues before Focusing together.

You might also decide upon a regular time to lead each other through Focusing, using either the basic Focusing steps or the guide to improving relationships. In addition, you may decide to structure your time together by taking turns or reversing roles at a later time so that the Focuser has an opportunity to digest the effects of a session before switching to become the guide.

At times, you may encounter difficulties for which outside assistance would be helpful. Do not expect to be able to work through every issue on your own or with your partner. Taking risks to ask for outside help can be a courageous step toward learning more about yourself and resolving obstinate barriers to intimacy.

APPENDIX G
A guide to separating

Breaking up is often one of the most painful human experiences. It is especially painful when trust has grown to support some significant degree of love and intimacy. The sense of panic or paralysis that often accompanies the first stage of separation may result from the loss of a person with whom we shared creative energies, be they sexual, emotional, intellectual, or spiritual.

A period of grieving is usually necessary in order to heal after separating from a meaningful relationship. Grieving primarily involves the experience and expression of our hurt. Anger is also frequently present. Giving appropriate expression to a full spectrum of emotions that arise can accelerate the process of letting go. For example, if we exclusively vent anger, we may fail to notice deeper undercurrents of sorrow and hurt. If, however, we are exclusively sad, we may neglect to be aware of the anger or rage that is also wanting recognition.

If a strong bond has been severed, or if we have been left in a harsh manner, we may need time to heal apart from the other person. Remaining friends may be a noble idea, but struggling to do so can seriously interfere with healing after a difficult separation. Re-stimulated by the other person's voice or presence, our wound may re-open, especially if he or she remains non-communicative.

Remaining friends is more possible when the wisdom of separating has been mutually recognized. Through a steady process of communicating feelings and discussing differences, mutual respect and understanding may grow to the point where separating may proceed in a friendly manner.

In relationships marked by a hostile or painful separation, we may, sometime later when it feels right, benefit from contacting the other person. Discussing what happened, if accompanied by a mutual willingness to admit limitations and weaknesses, could lead to much learning and healing for both individuals. The ability to really hear each other, perhaps for the first time, could lead to an experience of mutual forgiveness, followed by a new sense of closeness.

Whether we are initiating a separation or being left against our will, remaining open to the other person is very difficult. However, as we learn to befriend our hurt and take responsibility for our side of the interpersonal difficulty, we will be more capable of sharing honest feelings in a vulnerable way. Conflict can be reduced through approaching one another with maximum awareness and sensitivity. Then, rather than seeing the relationship as a meaningless tragedy, the experience of separating can be used to become clearer about what we really want and what does not work for us.

The following guide is intended to help you become clearer about your feelings and needs during a time of separation. You may use this guide by yourself or with a facilitator when you are considering separating or have been left by another person. It is to be used in conjunction with the basic Focusing steps on page 167.

PREPARATION
Take some time to become quiet. . . (pause). Allow your attention to settle inside your body. . .

1 NOTICING HOW YOU FEEL
Allowing your attention to remain inside your body, notice how the whole situation with ———— (say the person's name) feels right now. . . (pause). (If not much is coming, do you notice anything you're feeling upset or disappointed about? Is there anything you're missing?. . . Or, say to yourself, 'I'm feeling really fine about this whole thing, aren't I?').

When something comes, proceed to step 3 of the basic Focusing steps on page 168. If you feel stuck at some point or want to explore other issues related to separating, you may notice what comes in response to one of the following questions. If something then arises, just stay with your felt sense of that, returning to step 4a of the Focusing steps.

- Allowing your attention to remain inside your body, notice if there's anything you want to communicate that would help you feel more complete.
- Are there any resentments you would like to express? Any feelings of appreciation?
- Do you have a sense of what was missing for you that you would like to have in your next involvement?
- Do you have a sense of what you learned from the relationship?
- How would it feel to remain friends?

The following questions may be especially helpful if you are considering initiating the separation. Remember to allow your attention to rest inside your body as you Focus on each question.

- Can you accept the differences that exist between you?
- Can you accept this person as he or she is and still remain involved?
- Is there anything more you could learn by staying in the relationship?
- Does anything need to change within yourself in order to feel better about the relationship?

APPENDIX H
Some words that convey feelings

Fear/anxiety
horrified
panicky
terrified
dreadful
paralyzed
hysterical
scared
afraid
desperate
intimidated
threatened
apprehensive
pressured
uptight
nervous
edgy
jittery
worried
trembling
hesitant
tense
shy
agitated
freaked-out
contracted
distraught
frightened

Sensory feeling words
shaky
jumpy

jittery
constricted
tense
pressure
crampy
hard
cold
hot
warm
frozen
knotted
heavy
light
dull
bubbly
achy
heavy
sticky
ragged
tingly
sick
nauseous

Guilt/shame
humiliated
embarrassed
exposed
ashamed
guilty
regretful
small
remorseful

Angry
enraged
furious
infuriated
hateful
bitter
hostile
resentful
disgusted
annoyed
perturbed
dismayed
irked
irritated
impatient
frustrated
pissed-off
aggravated

Sad
discouraged
melancholy
grief
anguish
despair
dejected
hopeless
bleak
distressed
miserable
upset
wistful
sorrow
tearful
horrible
blue
down
disappointed
sorry
heavy
despondent

Lonely
abandoned
isolated
disconnected
alone
cut off
estranged
removed
left out
aloof
bored
distant
lonesome
longing
desirous
alienated

Hurt
betrayed
unappreciated
wounded
abused
crushed
pain
devastated
depreciated
anguish
used
devalued
neglected
minimized

Contented
enthusiastic
ecstatic
blissful
thrilled
enthralled
amused
elated
excited
open
euphoric

delighted
happy
cheerful
pleasure
free
glad
good
gratified
fine
wonderful
confident
serene
quiet
at peace
tranquil
relaxed
centered
balanced
alive
relieved
fulfilled
satisfied

Connected
tenderness
love
affection
intimate
devotion
cherish
caring
respect
closeness
warmth
like
trust
concern
friendly
in contact

in touch
accepted
united
supported
nourished
appreciated
gratitude
shy
kindness
compassion

Others
uncomfortable
powerless
helpless
disoriented
weak
puzzled
perplexed
troubled
envious
jealous
discomforting
doubtful
tired
overwhelmed
exhausted
fatigued
worn-out
lethargic
distrustful
giddy
curious
astonished
wonder
surprised
inspired
courageous
stimulated

APPENDIX I
A guide to resources

We are developing a growing network of counselors, therapists, and educators whose approach is harmonious with the perspective presented in this book. We may be able to recommend a practitioner in your area. We also offer groups, and trainings in the San Francisco area for professionals and the general public. If you would like to request a referral to a practitioner in your vicinity, or would like more information about our trainings or groups, please send a self addressed, stamped envelope to John and Kris Amodeo, P.0. Box 5100, Larkspur Landing Station, Larkspur, California 94939–5100.

The following is our most current list of individuals who offer either Focusing workshops, counseling, or education that is consistent with or complementary to our personal growth perspective. You may write to us for a more updated list.

UNITED STATES
Alaska

Linda Webber
880 H Street No. 208
Anchorage, Alaska 99501
(907) 276–4910

California

Los Angeles

Joseph Tein, M.A., MFCC
1535 Stoner Ave.
Los Angeles, Ca. 90025
(213) 826–9129

Orange County

Karen Bohan, M.A., MFCC
801 Glenneyre Suite F
Laguna Beach, Ca. 92651
(714) 494–5858

San Diego Area

Pat Rice, Ph.D.
Center for Studies of the Person
1125 Torrey Pines Road
La Jolla, Ca. 92037
(619) 459–3861

San Francisco Bay Area and
Napa County

John Amodeo, Ph.D.
Kris Amodeo, M.A,
P.0. Box 5100
Larkspur Landing Station
Larkspur, Ca. 94939–5100
(415) 388–9709

Santa Barbara

Dawn George, M.A., MFCC
888 San Ysidro Lane
Santa Barbara, Ca. 93108
(805) 969–5396

Brad Parks, M.A., MFCC
100 North Hope Ave. No 16
Santa Barbara, Ca. 93110
(805) 687–5491

Illinois

Reva Bernstein
1341 Jamie Lane
Homewood, Illinois 60430
(312) 798–2090

Rosemary Duncan, r.c.
513 Fullerton Parkway
Chicago, Illinois, 60614
(312) 528–6300

Eugene Gendlin, Ph.D
University of Chicago
5848 S. University Ave.
Chicago, Illinois 60637
(312) 962–8869

Massachusetts

Kent Poey, Ph.D.
20 Gatehouse Road
Amherst. Mass. 01002
(413) 253–3210

Ruth McGoldrick, S.P., M.R.E.
Elizabeth Oleksak, S.P., L.P.N.
53 Mill Street
Westfield, Massachusetts 01085
(413) 562–3627

Missouri

Marilyn Wussler, S.S.N.D., M.A.
320 E. Ripa Avenue
St. Louis, Missouri 63125
(314) 544–0455

Mississippi

Lisa Shapiro, M.S.W.
Rt. 1 Box 554
Oxford, Mississippi 38655
(601) 234–7684

New Jersey

George Fritz, Ed. D.
2D Seber Road
Hackettstown, New Jersey
07840
(215) 866–4360

New York

Neil Solomon, Ph.D.
24 Shore Park Road
Great Neck, New York 11023
(516) 487–5226

Ohio

James Kantner, Ph. D.
Diocesan Consultation Center
5201 Airport Highway
Toledo, Ohio 43615
(419) 385–5701

Pennsylvania

George Fritz, Ed. D.
1600 Lehigh Parkway East
Allentown, Pennsylvania 18103
(215) 866–4360

Texas

Marshall Rosenberg, Ph. D.
3229 Bordeaux
Sherman, Texas 75090
(214) 893–3886

Elfie Hinterkopf, Ph.D.
4159 Steck Avenue, Apt 294
Austin, Texas 78759
(512) 343–1613

BELGIUM

Mia Leijssen
Bosduifweg 9
2850 Keerbergen
(016) 22 06 64

CANADA

Queen of Apostles Renewal
Center
2165 Mississauga Rd.
Mississauga, Ontario L5H 2K8

ENGLAND

Beverley and Barbara McGavin-
Edwards
43 Oriel Grove
Southdown
Bath, Avon BA2 1JE
Bath (0225) 337162

David Garlovsky, M.A.
38 Bayston Road
London N16 7LT
01–254–6355

GERMANY

Dr Johannes Wiltschko
Markstrasse 8
D-8000 München 40
089 333538

JAPAN

Akira Ikemi
University of Occupational and
Environmental Health
Yahata Nishiku 807
093 603–1611

Shoji Murayama, Ph.D.
Faculty of Education
Kyushu University 03
6–19–1 Hakozaki Higashi-ku
Fukuoka

SWITZERLAND

Dr Agnes Wild-Missong
8032 Zurich
Kreuzplatz
01–69 48 50

THE NETHERLANDS

Bart Santen, Ph. D.
Reiendonk 25
4824 CC Breda
076–410214

SPAIN

Carlos Alemany, Ph. D.
Departmento de Psicologia
Universidad Pontificia
Comillas
Madrid–28049

The following periodicals and newsletters are also available:

The Focusing Folio
Fine Arts Building Suite 212
410 South Michigan Ave
Chicago, Illinois 60605

The Focusing Connection
5825 Telegraph Ave #45
Oakland, Ca. 94609

For a newsletter and pamphlets on Focusing and spirituality, contact:

Peter Campbell, Ph.D.
Ed McMahon, Ph.D.
6305 Greeley Hill Rd.
Coulterville, Ca. 95311

Notes

CHAPTER 4 THE WILLINGNESS TO BE VULNERABLE

1 For more on this theme, see the best-selling book by T. Peters, *In Search of Excellence*, New York, Harper & Row, 1982.

CHAPTER 5 FOCUSING: A PROCESS OF BEING WITH OUR FELT EXPERIENCE

1 Psychologist Norman Don's research is discussed in the *Journal of Altered States of Consciousness*, 1977–78, 3 (2), pp. 147–68.

CHAPTER 6 THE FOCUSING STEPS

1 Open-ended questions are ones that allow a wide range of possible responses. For example, we might ask, 'How are you feeling,' rather than, 'Are you angry?'
2 Each teacher of Focusing may present the steps in a slightly different form, according to his or her own experience of what seems to be most effective. As you become more familiar with Focusing, the formal steps become less important than the quality of attention you bring to your presently felt experience.
3 S. Suzuki, *Zen Mind, Beginner's Mind*, New York, Weatherhill, 1970, p. 31.
4 Adrian van Kaam conveys this sentiment well: 'I can be gentle with myself if I can experience myself simultaneously as precious and vulnerable' ('Anger and the Gentle Life,' in J. Welwood (ed.), *Awakening the Heart*, Boulder, New Science Library, 1983, p. 92).

CHAPTER 7 REPLACING THE INNER CRITIC WITH AN INNER CARETAKER

1 This term is described by poet-scholar Kenneth Cohen in an article entitled, 'The Tea Ceremony,' from *Yoga Journal*, March/April, 1978.

CHAPTER 8 TRUST: A FOUNDATION FOR INTIMACY

1 C.Rogers, *Person to Person: The Problem of Being Human*, Lafayette, Ca., Real People Press, 1967, p. 91.
2 Rogers, ibid., pp. 24–5.
3 A 1985 Gallup pole conducted in the US indicates that 66 percent of the public has a 'great deal' or 'quite a lot' of confidence in the church or organized religion (quoted from the *San Francisco Chronicle*, July 15, 1985).
4 An excellent book describing a psychologically sound approach to spirituality is *Biospirituality: Focusing As a Way to Grow* By P. Campbell and E. McMahon. In another book by the same authors entitled *Please Touch*, they state on p. 41, 'God is as close to us as we can risk being close to our real selves.'
5 For an excellent discussion of the harmful power dynamics that can occur between helping professionals and their clients, see *Power in the Helping Professions* by Adolph Guggenbühl-Craig, Dallas, Spring Books, 1971.

CHAPTER 9 SELF-REVEALING COMMUNICATION: A VITAL BRIDGE BETWEEN TWO WORLDS

1 Dr Martin L. Hoffman, a developmental psychologist at the University of Michigan, summarizes this research as follows: 'The data strongly suggests that empathy is part of the developmental foundation for the child's future system of moral behavior, as well as for the social behaviors such as altruism and sharing.' (Quoted from the article by J. Alper, 'The Roots of Morality,' *Science 85* March, 1985)

CHAPTER 10 A GUIDE TO EFFECTIVE COMMUNICATION

1 A helpful resource in this regard is a book by Robert Bolton, Ph. D., *People Skills*, Englewood Cliffs, N.J., Prentice Hall, 1979.

Another useful book is by Marshall B. Rosenberg, *A Model for Nonviolent Communication*, Philadelphia, New Society Publishers, 1983.

CHAPTER 11 WORKING WITH ANGER

1   D. Wile, *Couples Therapy – a Nontraditional Approach*, New York, John Wiley, 1981, p. 12.

Bibliography

Alper, J., 'The roots of morality,' *Science 85*, March, 1985.

Amodeo, J., 'The complementary effects of meditation and Focusing,' Ph.D. dissertation, California Institute of Transpersonal Psychology, 1981a.

Amodeo, J., 'Focusing applied to a case of disorientation in meditation,' *Journal of Transpersonal Psychology*, 1981b, vol. 13, no. 2.

Becker, E., *The Denial of Death*, New York: The Free Press, 1973.

Bolton, R., *People Skills*, Englewood Cliffs, N.J.: Prentice-Hall, 1979.

Brooks, C., *Sensory Awareness*, New York: Viking Press, 1974.

Bugental, J.F.T., *Psychotherapy and Process: The Fundamentals of an Existential-Humanistic Approach*, Reading: Wesley Publishing Co., 1978.

Campbell, P., and McMahon, E., *Biospirituality: Focusing as a Way to Grow*, Chicago: Loyola University Press, 1985.

Campbell, S., *Beyond the Power Struggle*, San Luis Obispo, Ca.: Impact Publishers, 1983.

Cohen, K., 'The tea ceremony,' *Yoga Journal*, March/April, 1978.

Don, N.S., 'The transformation of conscious experience and its EEG correlates,' *Journal of Altered States of Consciousness*, 1977–1978, vol 3, no. 2, pp. 147–68.

Ellis, A., and Harper, R.A., *A New Guide to Rational Living*, Hollywood: Wilshire Book Co., 1975.

Egendorf, A., and Jacobson, L, 'Teaching the very confused to make sense: an experiential approach to modular training with psychotics,' *Psychiatry*, vol. 45, no. 4, November 1982.

Friedman, N., *Experiential Therapy and Focusing*, New York: Half Court Press, 1982.

Gendlin, E.T., 'A theory of personality change,' in P. Worchel and D. Byrne (eds), *Personality Change*, New York: Wiley, 1964.

Gendlin, E. T., Beebe J., Cassens, J., Klein, M., and Oberlander, M., 'Focusing ability in psychotherapy, personality, and creativity,' in

J. Shlein (ed.), *Research in psychotherapy III*, Washington, D.C.: American Psychological Association, 1967.

Gendlin, E.T., 'Focusing,' *Psychotherapy: Theory, Research, and Practice*, 1969, vol 6, no. 1.

Gendlin, E.T., 'A theory of personality change,' in A. Mahrer (ed.), *Creative Developments in Psychotherapy*, Cleveland: Case Western Reserve, 1971.

Gendlin, E.T., 'Experiential psychotherapy,' in R. Corsini (ed.), *Current Psychotherapies*, Ithaca, Ill.: F.E. Peacock Publishers, 1973.

Gendlin, E.T., *Focusing*, New York: Bantam Books, 1981.

Gordon, T., *Parent Effectiveness Training*, New York: New American Library, 1975.

Guggenbühl-Craig, A., *Power in the Helping Professions*, Dallas: Spring Books, 1971.

Hinterkopf, E., and Brunswick, L.K., 'Teaching therapeutic skills to mental patients,' *Psychotherapy: Theory, Research, and Practice*, 1975.

Hinterkopf, E., and Brunswick, L., 'Promoting interpersonal interaction among mental patients by teaching them therapeutic skills,' *Psychosocial Rehabilitation Journal*, Spring, 1979.

Leonard, G.B., *Education and Ecstasy*, New York: Dell Publishing, 1968.

Lowen, A., *Pleasure*, New York: Penguin Books, 1975.

Maslow, A., 'Neurosis as a failure of personal growth,' *Humanitas*, 1967, vol 3, pp. 153–69.

Maslow, A., *Toward a Psychology of Being*, New York: D. Van Nostrand Co., 1968.

Maslow, A., *The Farther Reaches of Human Nature*, New York: Viking Press, 1971.

May, R., Angel, A., and Ellenderger, H.F. (eds), *Existence*, New York: Simon & Schuster, 1958.

McMahon, E. and Campbell, P., *Please Touch*, Mission, Kansas: Sheen & Ward, 1969.

Moustakas, C.E., *Loneliness*, Englewood Cliffs, N.J.: Prentice-Hall, 1961.

Peck, M.S., *The Road Less Traveled*, New York: Simon & Schuster, 1978.

Peters, T.J., *In Search of Excellence*, New York: Harper & Row, 1982.

Rogers, C., *On Becoming a Person*, Boston: Houghton-Mifflin, 1961.

Rogers, C., *Client-centered Therapy*, Boston: Houghton-Mifflin, 1965.

Rogers, C. and Stevens, B., *Person to Person: The Problem of Being Human*, Lafayette, Ca.: Real People Press, 1967.

Rosenberg, M.B., *A Model for Non-violent Communication*, Philadelphia: New Society Publishers, 1983.

Roszak, T., *Person/Planet*, Garden City, N.Y.: Anchor Press/Doubleday, 1979.

Roth, G., *Feeding the Hungry Heart*, New York: Bobbs-Merrill, 1982.

Satin, M., *New Age Politics*, New York: Dell Publishing, 1978.

Small, J., *Transformers: Therapists of the Future*, Marina del Rey, Cal.: De Vorss, 1982.

Suzuki, S., *Zen Mind, Beginner's Mind*, New York: Weatherhi11, 1970.

Teilhard de Chardin, P., *Building the Earth*, Wilkes-Barre, Pa: Dimension Books, 1965.

Teilhard de Chardin, P., *The Phenomenon of Man*, New York: Harper & Row, 1959.

Tenov, D., *Love and Limerance*, New York: Stein & Day, 1979.

Van Kaam, A., 'Anger and the gentle life,' in J. Welwood (ed.), *Awakening the Heart*, Boulder: New Science Library, 1983.

Walsh, R., *Staying Alive*, Boulder: New Science Library, 1984.

Weiss, J., 'The effects of meditation on experiential focusing,' Ph.D. dissertation, Northwestern University, 1978.

Welwood, J., 'Reflections on psychotherapy, focusing, and meditation,' *Journal of Transpersonal Psychology*, 1980, vol. 12, no. 2.

Welwood, J. (ed.), *Awakening the Heart*, Boulder: New Science Library, 1983.

Wilber, K., *No Boundary*, Los Angeles: Center Publications, 1979.

Wile, D.B., *Couples Therapy, A Nontraditional Approach*, New York: John Wiley, 1981.

Yutang, Lin, *The Importance of Living*, New York: John Day Co., 1937.

INDEX

acceptance: of another's world, 148–51; attitude of, 12, 42, 59, 178; of feelings, 13, 72, 148; need for, 90–91; of self, 90

addictions: romantic love, 20;substances, 32, 105

advertising, effects of, 11, 14

altered states of consciousness, 173

anger: beliefs about, 22; 'clean' expression of, 138–43; 'destructive' expression of, 138; effects when suppressed, 9–10, 21–2, 44–5, 136; expression of, 44, 68, 136–43; release of, 140; responding to, 143; women and, 9

assumptions regarding others, 132–5

barriers to Focusing, 57, 68, 170–5, 181–2

being with issues, 54, 56–7; difficulty with, 55, 58, 170–3

being seen, 87, 89, 95–6

beliefs: anger and, 9–10, 22, 137; effects of, 86; faith, 84–6, 100; irrational, 131; romantic love, 15, 17, 158; systems, 10, 33, 41, 84–5, 137, 147

betrayal, 20, 76, 156, 158–61

biofeedback, 46

BMR's (Basic Minimum Requirements), 183–5

bodily: felt experience, 27, 58–9; felt insight, 3; felt sense, 44–5, 58–9, 60; felt shift, 46; physiological release, 46, 47, 49, 59, 60, 140, see also felt shift

body armor, 58; see also muscular armor

body language, 110

brain wave patterns, 46

Campbell, S., 183

Capitalism, 92

caretaker, see inner caretaker

caretaking statements, 129

'checking' Focuser, 180

checking out assumptions, 132–5

childhood, 39–40, 105; needs, 8–9, 10, 33, 40; psychoanalysis and, 48; rejection, 8, 67

children, traits of, 39–40

Christianity, 99–101; and sin, 103–4

'clean' anger, 138–43

commitment: to accept others, 148–51; 'formal', 144; and marriage, 144–6, 155–7;

process, 144; to self-
  actualization, 146
communication: checking out
  assumptions, 132–5;
  congruent, 88–9, 146; critical,
  131–2; effective, 109–11,
  121–35; honesty and, 87–9;
  language and, 111–14;
  minimizing distractions to,
  115; of needs, 36; nonverbal,
  110, 178; non-violent, 164;
  responsibility for, 20,
  114–15; see also self-revealing
  communication
Communism, 92
conditioning, 13, 14, 17, 40; see
  also socialization
congruence, 78, 79, 88–9, 91,
  146
control: anger and, 9–10, 138; in
  beliefs, 85–6; in feelings, 10,
  67, 85; in Focusing process,
  58; relinquishing, 12, 36–8, 46,
  86, 93, 94, 100
counterdependence, 10
courageous, definition of, 84
critic, see inner critic
critical beliefs, 85
critical communication, 131–2
cultural beliefs, 14, 17, 33

dependency: in childhood and
  infancy, 8; fear of, 10–11; on
  others, 20, 102, 157
'destructive' anger, 138–43
disarmament, 163

Ellis, A., 131
empathy, 95, 114, 148, 177
engagement, process of, 151–2
evaluative statements, 122, 128
evolutionary perspective, 99
experiential therapy, 52

exploratory questions, 63, 169,
  180

faith, 84–6, 100, 105
'falling in love', 15–16, 17
feedback (from Focusing
  session), 177, 179
felt experience: communicating
  with others, 28, 109;
  definition of, 27; engaging
  others, 152; and Focusing, 42,
  43, 61, 63–4, 66; invalidating,
  28–9; mistrust of, 67; of
  needs, 29–33; opening to,
  69–70, 74, 147; vulnerability
  and, 38
felt meanings, 28–29, 47, 62–3,
  124
felt needs, 29–35, 41, 125
felt sense, 44–5, 47, 60;
  expression of, 59–62, 168–9;
  formation of, 58–9, 168
felt shift, 46, 60, 62, 172–4, 190
'fight or flight' response, 118
Focuser, 176, 189
Focusing, 2, 42–65; on anger,
  68; allowing a felt sense to
  form, 58–9; barriers to, 57,
  68, 170–5, 181–2; in caring
  for self, 71–2; clearing a space
  for, 53–5, 69, 167;
  communication and, 109, 121,
  123–4; definition of, 2;
  essence of, 43; expectations
  and, 47, 174; eye position
  during, 53, 171, 173; feedback
  from process, 177–9;
  identification of issues, 53–5;
  inventory, taking, 53–5, 167,
  187–8; meditation and, 53;
  outcomes, 50; pacing the
  Focusing session, 177, 181;
  preparation for, 52–3, 167,
  194; separating, guide to,

194–5; sensing importance of issues, 55–6, 278; steps, 2, 42, 43, 45, 52–65, 167–9, 185, 187–8
forgiveness, 75–6, 78
'formal' commitment, 144–6
forward moving questions, 63, 169, 174, 180
Freud, S., 30
Freudian analysis, 48
fundamentalist groups, 84

Gendlin, E., 2, 43, 52, 174
Gordon, T., 111
grace, 100
grieving: loss of relationship, 68, 160–1, 193; loss of romantic myths, 18
growth process, 49
guide, 176, 189
guide to: improving relationships, 186–8; initiating relationships, 183–5; resources, 2, 108, 196; separating, 193–5

haiku poetry, 77
healing, through close relationships, 108; through remorse, 77–9
hidden agendas, 90, 130
hierarchy of needs, 30; see also Maslow, A.
Hillel, R., 33
honesty, 87–9, 146–8
Humanistic Psychology, 30, 88

'I' statements, 112, 129
idealized mates, 14–16, 19
industrial psychologists, 11
inner: caretaker, 71–7, 90, 93, 94, 101, 102, 118, 183; child, 39–42, 70, 73, 96; critic, 9, 66–71, 72, 79, 150, 170, 171;

cynic, 66, 171, see also inner critic; intelligence, 11; process, 12; tension, 13, 59; voice, 9
integration of body and mind, 62
intellectual understanding, 3
intellectualizing, 58, 181
interactional system, 191
internal dialogue, 9
interpretive therapy, 52
intimacy: anger and, 143; creating, 13, 23, 39, 42, 74, 152; communication and, 111, 114; genuine, 15, 16, 159; marriage and, 146, 153–5; needs for, 31–2, 78, 84, 104; trust and, 87, 96, 100; vulnerability and, 40, 41
intrusive communication, 112–13, 117–18
inventory, 53–5, 167, 187–8
Ireland, 84
irrational beliefs, 131; see also Ellis, A.
issues: being with, 54; difficulty with, 58–9; identification of, 53–4, 167; sensing importance of, 55–6, 168; setting aside, 54–5; see also inventory; Focusing steps

'learning relationships', 183
life process, 102
listening, 178

marital contract, 146
marital union, 154, 160, see also union
marriage, 20, 145–8, 153–7, 158
Maslow, A., 30–1, 90, 162
meaning, see felt meaning
medical model, 106–7
meditation, 76; and Focusing, 53, 55, 173

meditative, 47, 173
memories, in Focusing process,
    59–60
Middle East, 84
monogamy, 184
muscular armor, 9, *see also* body
    armor

needs: for acceptance, 30, 90; for
    belonging, 8, 80; childhood,
    8–9, 33, 40; denial of, 33–4;
    felt needs, 29–35, 41, 125; for
    growth, 31, 33, 36; hierarchy
    of, 30; for intimacy, 31–2, 40,
    78, 84, 97, 104; recognition of,
    162; for support, 10
negative feelings, 21–2, 68, 74,
    90; avoidance of, 21, 68
nonverbal communication, 17,
    110, 178

Omega Point, 99
organismic contact, 96; *see also*
    being seen
organismic experience, 27–8, 32,
    35, 55, 97, 99, 100
organismic needs, 79; *see also* felt
    needs

pacing Focusing questions, 177
Parent Effectiveness Training,
    111
parental demands, 8, 67
passive-aggressive behavior, 137
peace, global, 111, 162–5
personal growth: crises and, 12;
    definition of, 1; Focusing and,
    65; relationships and, 19, 21,
    118; in work environments,
    37
personality patterns, 11
physical symptoms of repressed
    feelings, 9, 21, 136

present: as a way of being, 44,
    119; sense of, 49, 53
'process' approach to marriage,
    157
'process' commitment, 144
psychoanalysis, 48
psychotherapy, 1, 43

Rational-Emotive therapy, 131
recycling Focusing steps, 61
referrals, *see* guide to resources
reflection, 179
rejection, 8, 41, 67, 75, 105, 159
relationships: anger, expressing,
    22, 143; commitment,
    144–57; Focusing steps for
    improving, 186–8; Focusing
    steps for initiating, 183;
    grieving loss of, 68, 160–1,
    193; honesty and, 87–8;
    initiating, 1, 7, 13, 18, 183–5;
    life experience, to, 46;
    marriage and, 145–57;
    remorse, and, 76; separating
    from, 98, 147, 160, 193–4;
    spirituality and, 99, 101–4;
    therapeutic, 105–8
relearning trust, 105
religion, 33, 84–5, 103
remorse, 76, 77–9, 99, 147
repeating, 179
resources, guide to, 2, 108, 196
respect, 91–5
'responsibility athlete', 10
risks: of growth, 106; in
    relationships, 74, 78, 85–7,
    100, 114; in vulnerability, 41,
    78, 105
Rogers, C., 88, 96, 99
romantic myths, 14–23; 'falling
    in love', 15–16, 17; marriage
    and, 155, 158; social
    conditioning, 14–17

self-actualization, 31, 69, 76, 102, 145, 146, 159, 160, 162
self-affirmation, 7, 74, 79, 150
self-critical thoughts, 8, 9
self-esteem, 18, 31, 90, 156
self-revealing communication, 109–20, 129, 139
sense of community, 37
separation from relationships, 98, 147, 160, 193–4
sexual pleasure, 100
sin, 103
social issues, 93, 163
socialization, effects of, 66
sorrow, 77
spirituality, 99–104
steps to Focusing, 2, 42, 43, 45, 52–65, 167–9, 187–8, 194–5
stressful life situations, 12, 72
surrendering: to feelings, 72; to others, 86; personal power, 15, 18; sexuality and, 100
survival, 11, 33, 36, 37, 99, 105, 164
Suzuki, S., 54

Teilhard de Chardin, 99, 102, 103, 104
therapeutic relationship, 105–8
therapists: referrals, *see* guide to resources; selection of, 105–6
Thoreau, H. D., 31
Thornbirds, 20
tips for the Focusing guide, 176–82
transformative effects of feeling, 118

Transpersonal Psychology, 30
trouble-shooting reference guide, 170–5
trust: barriers to, 105; blind trust, 87, 158; in Focusing, 56; ingredients of, 87–96; in life, 101–4; loss of, 109; in relationships, 39, 186; relearning, 104–5; in self, 73–5, 86, 94, 101–4; with others, 86–7, 91, 97, 101–4
trust-promoting: environments, 94, 105, 115; values, 98–9

union, sense of, 119, 144, 153–4, 156, 158
University of Chicago, 2, 43
unlayering, 64
unwanted emotions, 67; *see also* negative emotions

value directions, 96–7
vulnerability: and control, 36–8; in expressing anger, 142; and felt experience, 38; needs, 40; opening to, 40, 78; power of, 116; recognition of, 38; risks, 41

Western medicine, 106; *see also* medical model
wholeness, 78
Wile, D., 139–40
workplace, transformation of, 36–8

'you' statements, 112